THE HOWLING
WASTELANDS

THE HOWLING
WASTELANDS

PATRICIA MEYER

TATE PUBLISHING
AND ENTERPRISES, LLC

Published by Tate Publishing & Enterprises, LLC
127 E. Trade Center Terrace | Mustang, Oklahoma 73064 USA
1.888.361.9473 | www.tatepublishing.com

Tate Publishing is committed to excellence in the publishing industry. The company reflects the philosophy established by the founders, based on Psalm 68:11,
"The Lord gave the word and great was the company of those who published it."

Book design copyright © 2015 by Tate Publishing, LLC. All rights reserved.
Cover design by Maria Louella Mancao
Interior design by Manolito Bastasa

Published in the United States of America

ISBN: 978-1-68142-114-8
1. Family & Relationships / Death, Grief, Bereavement
2. Family & Relationships / Marriage & Long Term Relationships
15.03.30

"He found him in a desert land, and in the waste howling wilderness; he led him about, he instructed him, he kept him as the apple of his eye."

—Deuteronomy 32:10

CONTENTS

PREFACE

This is one woman's story of her journey through the wilderness. It is a story of God's providential grace and mercy. It is my story.

My life's story isn't one of perfection. It isn't one full of wisdom. It is a life full of mistakes, heartaches, and tears. Yet by God's great mercy and endless grace, it has become one of promise and wonder.

My desire in writing my story is to glorify God and possibly help another to see that God is able to take us from a wasteland of a life and guide us through the wilderness into His promised land. The verses God gave me are what I hold on to for my promises, and they are coming true, even today. They're found in Ezekiel 36.

> And I will multiply men upon you, all the house of Israel, even all of it; and the cities shall be inhabited, and the wastes shall be built:
>
> And I will multiply upon you man and beast; and they shall increase and bring fruit: and I will settle you after your old estates, and will do better unto you than at your beginnings: and ye shall know that I am the Lord. (Ezekiel 36:10–11)
>
> Thus saith the Lord God; In the day that I shall have cleansed you from all your iniquities I will also cause you to dwell in the cities, and the wastes shall be built. (Ezekiel 36:33)

Then the heathen that are left round about you shall know that I the Lord build the ruined places, and plant that that was desolate: I the Lord have spoken it, and I will do it. (Ezekiel 36:36)

To God be the glory for the great thing He has done! May you too find God's great grace and mercy fulfilled in your life. This is a story of reaping what we sow, but it shows how God restores the years the locust have stolen and works all things together for good to them who love Him and are called according to His purpose. I have no great call, except that of wife, mother, and grandmother. Yet it all began with being a daughter.

1

BUILDING SAND CASTLES

"And everyone that hears these sayings of mine, and does them not, shall be likened unto a foolish man, which built his house upon the sand: and the rain descended, and the floods came, and the winds blew, and beat upon that house; and it fell: and great was the fall of it."

—Matthew 7:26–27

CHAPTER 1

I was fifteen when I met Walt. We were living in La Verne California and attending Bonita High School. I loved living in Southern California. The sun shines nearly all year round. From La Verne, the Sierra Mountains are just an hour drive in one direction; and the Pacific Coast, an hour drive in the other direction. It has abundant greenery with palm trees as well as evergreens, and there are flowers in bloom all year round.

La Verne is a small town in the Pamona Valley. It has a beautiful park called Kuhn's Park with a giant carob tree in the center of it that is over a hundred years old. It's large outstretched gnarly branches was a favorite place that we would climb up on and sit when we were young. It could hold a number of us all at once. I had grown up playing in that park, and Walt had moved in catty-corner from it when he was thirteen.

He was seventeen when he had asked me out, though he had noticed me before that. He told me once that there was a time when my friends and I were in Kuhn's Park and he and his friend Jerry were in his driveway working on a car, something Walt loved to do when he was in high school, like most boys at that age.

"Hey, Jerry," Walt said. "See those girls over in the park?" He was about to say that he was going to ask me out, but Jerry beat him to it.

"Yeah!" Jerry replied. "I'm going to ask out the blonde! Her name is Patty, and her sister is friends with my sister. Her sister's name is Barbara Sherman. You know her. She's in your class."

Jerry was one year behind Walt in school, and I was two years. So Walt just mumbled, "Yeah, I know Barbara," in acknowledgment, but that was all. So Jerry later asked me out. That relationship didn't last long, and Walt was now able to pursue me.

I was fifteen and had blue eyes and long blond wavy hair parted down the middle. I usually dressed in blue jeans or cut-off shorts and T-shirts or tank tops. I walked around barefoot, even at school, although it wasn't allowed. It might seem that I didn't have much respect for authority, but in reality, I was just trying to be the cool girl that I thought I was.

On a warm day in October, while walking to my locker between classes, Walt walked up to me and asked if I wanted to go to the football game with him that night. I only noticed how big in the shoulders he was as he approached. His hands seemed clenched, and his friends Mike and Rick were in the background acting like monkeys. I had just finished upsetting a girl by threatening her because she had insulted my friend. I thought the girl had sent Walt to punch me or something, so when he had finished asking me out, I told him no, that I was on restriction, which I was. I went over and told my friends that Walt had just asked me out.

"What did you say?" asked Vicki.

"I said no!" I told her.

"Why did you do that?" exclaimed Donna.

"He's goofy looking, and besides, I'm on restriction," I replied.

"You can get off restriction, and he's cute!" exclaimed Donna again. "Besides, we want to go to the game. Just ask your mom, and she'll let you go. You always get off your restrictions."

"Yeah, but I already told him no. What if he sees me there?"

"That's your problem. We just want to go, and you probably won't run into him anyways. Just get off restriction, and we'll go to the game."

"How do you plan on getting there?" I asked.

"Doug can take us, can't he, Vicki?" Donna turned and questioned Vicki. Doug was Vicki's boyfriend, and he had his driver's license.

"Maybe. I'll ask him if he can," replied Vicki.

"Great. We'll call each other after we check with our moms, okay?" asked Donna.

"Yeah, sure," we each said then turned and went to our various classes.

Well, I was able to get my mom to let me go to the game, and Doug was happy to take all us girls. When we got there, we ran into Walt, Rick, and Mike. *Great!* I thought. I wanted to hide! I suggested we go to another bleacher, but come to find out, Donna liked Mike, so she wanted to go meet up with the guys. "But Walt's there, and I told him I was on restriction and couldn't come, remember?" I anxiously stated.

"That's your problem! We're going over there, right, Vicki?" Donna exclaimed.

Doug, who knew Walt and his buddies, spoke up and said, "Walt's a nice guy. He won't care. Come on, Patty. Let's go."

They started toward the group, and I lagged behind. Finally, I thought, *Why not go over there? Everyone is having a good time. I'll just sit and watch the game.*

I was really getting into the game. Our team, the Bearcats, was in need of a touchdown to win, and the ball was in their possession. The game was in the last minutes of the last quarter. The ball was snapped, and the quarterback was running down the field toward the goal. His teammates blocked one tackle after another. The quarter back then made a final leap into the air, over a missed tackle, and landed on the other side of the goal line. "Touch down!" exclaimed the announcer. The girls were hanging out at the top of the bleachers, on the walkway, with Doug, Mike, and Rick, I was sitting near the top; about four bleachers down; while Walt was sitting a couple of bleachers down from me.

I had stood up on the metal bleacher seat as I watched the play unfold. I became so excited when the touchdown was made that I started to jump on the bleacher seat. "We won! We won!" I exclaimed. While jumping and screaming, I came down and lost my footing. I fell headfirst down the bleachers. Walt had looked up at me as I was getting excited. He saw me fall and caught me before I hit the ground and broke my neck. He asked if I was all right. "Yes! Thanks for catching me," I said breathlessly. He just smiled. He wasn't mad at me for not going out with him. He never even mentioned it.

I looked up into his blue eyes and thought, *How could I have thought he wasn't cute?* He had blond hair, clear blue eyes, a wonderful smile, was so tanned and strong, and he had just saved my life! We talked as we walked down the bleachers through the gate and out into the parking lot. As I climbed into Doug's car, Walt asked, "Would you want to go out with me?"

"Sure! When?" I asked him.

"Can you go out tomorrow?" he questioned back.

"I'll ask my parents. Just call me tomorrow. Here's my phone number," I said as I quickly jotted down my number with a pen on the palm of his hand. My heart beat faster as I smiled up into his face, and he smiled a broad smile back as he looked down at my number and then made a fist as if to hold it tight. We said our good-byes then and headed our separate ways. "See, Patty?" Doug stated. "I told you Walt was a nice guy."

"Yeah!" I said dreamily. "He is." Then I sighed and watched him as we drove away.

"Mom!" I said excitedly as I came home. "A guy asked me out on a date for tomorrow night! His name is Walt Meyer, and I told him to call me and I'd let him know. Can I please go out with him? Please!" I pleaded.

"I don't know. Who is this guy?" she asked.

"Doug knows him," I said.

"So do I," injected Barbara, who was sitting at the kitchen table with Mom. "He's in my class, and he's a nice guy, Mom."

"Well, I'll have to talk it over with your father. We'll see," replied Mom.

I anxiously awaited both my father's answer and Walt's call. I was so excited and told Barbara so. "He's a real nice guy, Patty.

How did you guys meet?" she asked. I told her the whole story, and she had to laugh. "Your knight in shining armor!" she teased.

"Yeah!" I replied with a smile on my face and a lightness in my heart.

When Walt called that Saturday morning, I went to the phone in my bedroom. I told him I hadn't gotten an answer from my parents yet. "Well, can you find out?" he asked.

"Sure, hold on." I put the phone down and went to ask.

I found both my parents sitting at the kitchen table drinking coffee and going over the grocery list. With ten mouths to feed, my parents went shopping every Saturday. A chore they did not look forward to.

"Dad, Mom," I started, "would it be all right if I went out with Walt? Remember I asked you last night, Mom?"

"Yes, that's right," she said. "Russ, Patty would like to go out with a guy named Walt tonight. Barbara knows him from her class, and she said he's nice."

"When and where?" asked Dad.

"I don't know," I replied.

"Well, don't you think you should find out?" he stated.

"Oh! Yeah!" I exclaimed. So I headed back to the bedroom to pick up the phone, but Mom said, "Answer it here."

"But I already have the phone off the hook in my bedroom," I said.

"That's okay. Answer it in here." So I picked up the phone on the kitchen wall and asked Walt where he was planning to take me.

"I thought we'd go out to eat first then a movie, if that's all right," he answered.

"I don't know about a movie, but going out to eat is fine and what time?" questioned Dad after I let him know what Walt had said. I was a bit disappointed but relayed to Walt what my father had said. "That's fine. I can pick you up around 6 p.m. Is that okay with your dad?" he asked. So I asked my father, and he said that would be fine. My mom sat there with a bit of a smile on her face.

I spent the rest of the day with my friend Vicky, telling her about my upcoming date. This was Vicky Vessel, my friend from my neighborhood as well as school. She hadn't been able to go to the game with us, so I excitedly filled her in on all the details of the previous night.

"How romantic!" she exclaimed.

"Yeah, and he's so cute and so sweet!" I told her.

"So what are you going to wear?" she asked then began a frantic look through my clothes and my sister's clothes too. I sometimes borrowed my sister's clothing because she was older and had such cool clothes!

Well, the time finally came, and Walt drove up to my house in his baby blue 1962 Chevy Nova. Vicky, whose father worked on restoring cars, exclaimed, "What a cool car! I can't believe he's driving a '62 Nova!"

"I hadn't known what kind of car he drove. How neat!" I said. Then I ran out of my bedroom, where Vicky and I had been watching from my window. "Mom! Dad! Walt's here. Can I go now?"

"Hold on a minute," Dad said. "Have him first come in to meet us."

"What? Why!" I said in a raised voice. I didn't want him to have to come in. "Because if he's going to date my daughter, it's only right that he should come in and meet your father," Dad stated.

"Oh! Okay!" I said, a bit exasperated. So I went out and informed Walt that he'd have to come in and meet my parents first.

"I was just coming to get you," Walt said as he got out of his car. As we walked up to the front door, Walt opened it for me, something I told him he didn't have to do. We walked into the kitchen, where my parents were waiting.

"Hello. Walt, is it?" Dad asked. "Hello, Mr. Sherman, Mrs. Sherman. Yes, it's Walt," he replied.

"Well, it's nice to meet you. So where are you two kids going to eat?" Dad asked.

"I thought I'd take Patty out to Pondarosa," said Walt.

"Then what?" Dad asked again.

"Well, I thought maybe we'd drive around," he answered.

"Why don't you just come back here?" Dad said.

"What! Why?" I asked. Mom just looked at me sternly and said, "If you want to go out, that's what you'll do," she stated.

"That's fine, Mr. and Mrs. Sherman," replied Walt.

"When can we expect you back then?" questioned my dad.

"It shouldn't be too long. Around eight?" Walt hesitantly answered.

"Seven thirty sounds better," stated Dad. What were my parents trying to do? I couldn't understand any of this. They never had me do this before, but then again, this was my first date. I just sat there dumbfounded and upset.

So we went, and although it wasn't as long as I thought it should have been, we had a good time. When we came home by seven thirty, Walt and I sat outside, and some of my neighborhood friends and some of my siblings came up to meet him. Barbara came over and said hi to Walt.

"Cool car," she stated as she walked up to his car.

"Thanks," said Walt.

"Well, you better get inside, Patty," Barbara said. "Mom and Dad are waiting."

Walt walked me to the door and said good night.

"Good night," I said. "I had a great time."

"Me too. Can I see you again?" he asked.

"Wait! I'll ask," I replied and ran inside the house.

As I ran inside, I left him standing there on the doorstep. "Mom! Dad!" I exclaimed as I hurried into the living room, where they were sitting watching television. "Can I see him again?" I asked my parents.

"You'll see him in school, won't you?" questioned my mother with a bit of a smile.

"Yes, but what about going out again?" I asked.

"We'll worry about that later. You aren't going out on a school night anyways, so have him call you later," stated Dad.

"Can he come over during the week?" I asked.

"No! You have homework and chores to do after school," Mom said. "You'll see him in school, and that's enough for now."

So I went and told Walt what they had said. "Oh, okay," he said, a bit stunned. I stood there pouting. "It's fine. I'll see you at school then. Good night," he said as he looked deeply into my eyes.

"Good night, and thanks for a good time," I said, looking back into his blue eyes.

"You're welcome," he replied and turned with that and walked to his car and drove off into the night.

As I stepped inside, I stood for a minute and listened to the sound of his V-8 engine rumbling as he drove away. Mom came around the corner then and asked, "Well, did he kiss you good night?" she asked.

"No! Should he have? I didn't think you'd approve of that," I said.

"Well, we wouldn't care, but that's good. You should wait," was her reply. So began Walter's and my relationship. It would end up to be a special relationship, but I wouldn't realize just how special for a long time.

We dated for the rest of the school year. Our relationship wasn't what it should have been. We were promiscuous and deceitful to our parents. I had tried to approach my mother about my feelings for Walt before anything happened, but she wasn't listening.

"Mom, I think I'm in love with Walt," I had started.

"You don't know what love is," was her answer.

"But I really do love him!"

"It's just puppy love. You're too young to know what love is," was all she had to say.

I just got up and left. *What's the use? She never listens, and she won't talk with me. What am I going to do? I really have strong feelings for Walt. Mom, I really wish you would listen to me. Why won't you?* I wondered as I walked away.

Well, it didn't take us long to make the *big* step. I was the one who instigated it. Walt had already accepted me wanting to wait, and I think that's when I fell in love with him. It so impressed me that he was fine with just being with me. He had told me many times that he loved me, and I was sure I loved him.

All too soon, the end of the school year came, and the class of 1974 of Bonita High School was graduating. This included Walter and my sister Barbara, Rick, and Doug. We were all so excited! What a big day! Walt was looking forward to going to a mechanics school in Arizona that August and earning his mechanics degree, and Barbara was thinking of earning a nursing degree.

Walt had already proposed to me. He had written in my yearbook, "I love you and can't live without you. When you graduate and turn eighteen, will you marry me?"

"I love you so much! Yes, I will marry you! Will you wait for me?" I wrote in his. At that time, I was sixteen and Walt was eighteen. We were just kids but felt we were truly in love. We may have been, but we had no clue how that love could be tested by life and its difficulties we were about to face.

CHAPTER 2

We had a wonderful summer together. We went to the beach, Disneyland, and the California Jam concert. With every passing opportunity though, we continued in our sinful ways. We were so immature but were convinced we were doing what everyone else was; after all, what could possibly happen? We were taking precautions, like the clinic counselors told us as we had gone there earlier that year. We had it all under control. What young fools we were!

Well, the summer ended. Walt was soon going out of state to school. We were going to miss each other terribly.

"How am I going to do this?" Walt asked. "I can't live without you!"

"I feel the same way, babe," I said.

"Well, it won't be for long. We can call each other and write. I'll be coming home for the holidays too," he said, trying to encourage me.

"I'm worried you'll find someone else though," I sadly stated.

"You don't have to worry about that!" he said. "You're my wife, remember?"

This was something we had decided to secretly call one another—husband and wife—when I had broken down in tears after our first act of fornication.

It had happened six months earlier. Afterward, when we were in my home with everyone there, I started to cry softly.

"What's wrong?" Walt questioned me under his breath as he could see I was trying to hide it.

"I feel terrible!" I whispered. "We should never have done it, Walt. What if we break up? What if you leave me?"

He gently wrapped his arms around me and said, "That will never happen. I love you!"

"But we should have waited until we were married," I said under my breath, feeling every bit shameful.

He gently hugged me. "We should have, but you know that when two people do what we did, they are considered husband and wife," he quietly stated.

"They are?" I asked questionably.

"Yes," he said. "You are now my wife, and I am your husband."

I looked deep into his eyes and saw that he truly believed this even though it wasn't true. "Husband," I whispered as he dried my tears, "I love you!"

"I love you and always will. You are my wife now," he replied.

We were in love even if we were too young and immature to understand the seriousness of our actions.

The weather was changing, and there was change in the air for us all. It was now August of 1974, and soon, Walt would be off to his school in Arizona. High school would once again be starting for me as I was now in the eleventh grade, and later on in October, my dad would land a new job in Northern California. The family would have to move, which meant I'd be even farther from Walter.

The day came when Walt had to leave for Arizona. We had one more date and were saying our good-byes. I was so sad and scared. I had given myself completely to this guy. What if he found someone else while so far away? He might find someone prettier and older. I was so insecure.

"There will never be anyone but you," Walt said reassuringly as we sat in his newly painted, pearl white Nova. "I'm going to miss you so much, but I'm doing this for us so I can get a good-paying job to support you. Will you wait for me?"

"Yes, of course I will," I replied.

"You won't find someone else while I'm gone, will you?" he questioned me.

"No!" I said emphatically. "There will never be anyone but you in my life," I quoted him and smiled up into his blue eyes.

We kissed good night at my front door, and as he turned to get back in his car, I ran and grabbed him. "I can't stand it!" I cried.

"Me either," Walt said, and we just held each other. Then my mom came out and said I needed to come in the house. She told Walt we'd all miss him and said not to fret because we could talk on the phone and we'd see each other sooner than we thought. Her words were comforting as I stood there waving good-bye to Walt as he drove off in the night in his Nova. The next morning; he left for Arizona.

One day not too much later, as I was leaving with my friend, Vicky Vessel, and Barbara, my sister, who had decided to get me out of the house, Mom called out to me.

"Patty! Walt's on the phone, but I'll just tell him to call later."

"No!" I cried. "I want to talk with him! Please, Mom, can I?"

"I thought you were going out with the girls."

"Well, they can go without me. Go ahead, you guys. I want to talk with Walt," I stated.

"We can wait. Besides, I want to say hi too!" said Vicky Vessel. So I ran to the phone in my bedroom, and Vicky followed.

Vicky grabbed the phone and said, "Hi, Walt! What's it like in Arizona?" They talked a little until I grabbed the phone. Vicky said I was dying to talk with him and finally gave me the phone. When I said hi, I just started to cry. "I miss you so much! I wish you were here!"

"I wish I was there too!" said Walt. "I don't like it here. I'm not learning anything new. What I had hoped to learn, they send out to get done some place else. (Something to do with boring engines.) Besides, I miss you so much too! I'm coming home."

"Really? What about your schooling? Is that what you want?" I asked breathlessly.

"Yes! I'm going to call my parents and let them know. I'll be home as soon as I can arrange it."

"Oh, Walt! I love you!"

"I love you too!" he said.

"Walt's coming home!" I whispered to Vicky. I didn't go out that night as I sat and talked to Walt for another hour. Vicky and the others had left since it was obvious I wasn't going to get off the phone.

In a couple of weeks, Walt came home, his mother wasn't too happy with the decision, but she always stood by her boys no matter what. She wasn't real happy with me, and I could tell. I don't blame her. After all, she had high hopes for her son, and I was in the way of those hopes. Little did we know just how much.

I had been gaining weight, and my pants were getting tight. It was the beginning of October, and I realized I hadn't had a menstrual cycle since mid-August. I was scared and told my sister, Barbara. She had known about our actions because she had intercepted a letter from the free clinic shortly after I had gone there to get birth control pills.

"How long has it been since your last cycle?" she asked me.

"I had one in August but not since," I replied.

"You need to have a test done. I can take you to the clinic."

That was great of her to offer, but I wanted Walt to take me, and I told her so. "What if Walt doesn't want the baby," she stated. I had never even thought of that.

"He will!" I said nervously.

"You know you can get an abortion."

"I would never do that!"

"I hoped you would say that, but I had to be sure. Do you really think Walt will stick by you?"

"I think so."

"Well, you have to tell Walt then. If he can't take you to go get the test done, I will. And there's no need in telling Mom and Dad right now. You're not even sure." I hadn't even thought that far. So when Walt came over that night, as he did every night after work, I asked Mom if I could go out for a little while, and she said yes.

We had left my neighborhood and were driving down Bonita Ave.

"What's up?" asked Walt. "You seem quiet." I was quiet because I was deep in thought. I looked up at the maple trees as we drove down the treelined road. I really wasn't seeing the trees though, as I was deep in thought.

I might be pregnant, and I was sixteen. Of course, I knew this might happen, but they never tell you the odds when they're handing out the birth control. Yet, here I was, on the brink of a life-changing situation, not just for me but for Walt and now a new innocent baby's life as well.

After we had driven around for a while, I turned to Walt. He had been telling me something about his day at work, but I wasn't hearing him. As I looked at him smiling and talking away, I realized just how handsome and young he was, how young we both were. Would he really go through with all the promises he had made me? Would he be able to handle all the responsibility? Would he still love me? Those were the thoughts I was having as I gathered my courage to talk to him.

"Walt," I started, "I have something to tell you."

"What?" he questioned.

"This is important. Can we stop to talk?"

"Sure. What's up?" he said as he pulled the Nova over to the side of the road. I took a deep breath and said, "I think I'm pregnant."

There was a brief silence as he looked me in the eye.

"Are you serious?" he questioned.

"Serious," I said in a chocked voice. I hurried on, "I haven't had a cycle since August, and it's October now!"

"Really? What are we going to do?" he asked me. Like I knew! I swallowed hard and snidely replied, "I can have an abortion, you know."

"No!" he shouted. "You can't do that!"

"Yes, I can," I said.

"But it's my baby," Walt said sadly.

"Well, it's my body!" I shouted as I thought, *Don't you care about me? It's my baby too.* But instead, I coldly stated, "I don't have to have this baby, and you have nothing to say about it!"

Why am I acting this way, I thought. I want this baby, and I would never abort it. "Yeah, but just see if he really wants to marry you. He really doesn't have to, you know," a voice seemed to say to me. Well, I would soon find out the true character of Walter. Would he stand by me and this baby or not?

"Please, Patty!" he pleaded. "Don't get an abortion. I want this baby, and I want to marry you. We were planning on getting married anyways. We'll just get married sooner. You can't do this to me! Please!"

"You? What about me?" I answered.

After what seemed like a lifetime in silence, but in actuality, only a moment, I said, "I never would get an abortion. Besides, we don't even know if I am pregnant or not."

"How can we find out?" he asked me.

"Barbara said we can get a pregnancy test done at the clinic where we got the birth control."

"Okay. Let's go there tomorrow."

So it was settled. Walter did stand by me, and he did show me that he loved me. He was a boy soon to be put into a man's position, and he was willing; and soon enough, he would prove how able he was.

We didn't want my parents to find out, so Walt had taken off work and picked me up at school that day. He arrived on his Harley Davidson motorcycle he had just bought when he had come home from trade school. It was a beautiful bike. It had a seat big enough for us both to sit on, although my parents didn't want me on it. It was painted blue with metallic flakes in it. It sparkled in the Californian sunlight. He handed me his only helmet, and I put it on my head. I climbed on, and off we drove.

As we hummed down the freeway on the Harley, I could see the mountains and feel the breeze on my face. I was sitting up with my hands on Walt's waist, deep in thought. What was going to happen? I wasn't sure, and I was nervous and frightened. Walt was nervous as well; I'm sure. Would we be able to still be care-free teenagers, or would we have to take on the heavy load of parenthood? We would soon find out.

When we arrived at the clinic, we walked in, and I had to go to the desk and tell them I needed a pregnancy test. They gave me some forms to fill out and bring back to the desk. I did, and then the nurse gave me a cup and told me what to do with it and to bring it back when I was finished. I did, and then I went back to sit by Walt in the lobby with a large number of young girls and one other young guy. We waited to be called back for the results. It was the hardest thing we ever did! We realized that all these young girls were here for the same thing! Some looked scared, and yet others looked like it was no big deal. We were both scared to death!

When they called my name to give me the test results, Walt got up to go into the counseling with me.

"No!" the counselor said. "You can stay here."

"But I want him to come!" I said.

"Are you sure? He doesn't have to come."

"Yes!" I said.

"Well, you just don't say anything, you understand?" she told Walt.

"Yes," he said, then he took my hand, and we went in.

We walked into a small office, and she told us to shut the door and have a seat in front of her desk. As she sat on the other side of the desk, she looked at some papers in front of her. Then she looked up soberly at us and stated, "Well, the test is positive. You are pregnant." Our grasp tightened as Walt squeezed my hand tightly. We looked at each other in amazement.

"What do you want to do?" she asked me. "We can give you an abortion."

"No!" exclaimed Walt.

"Quiet, or you're out of here!" she sternly told Walt. Then turning back to me, she began again, "Ms. Sherman, as I was saying, we can schedule an abortion."

I immediately said, "No, I don't want one, and he can stay!"

"Well, what do you plan to do then?" she questioned.

"Well, I guess, tell my parents and take it from there," I said. "We'll get married!" Walt said in a gentle voice.

I turned and looked at him with fear in my eyes. He looked back at me with reassurance in his and said, "We were planning to anyways. We'll just get married now."

"That sounds great, but do you kids realize just how hard that will be? How will you take care of this baby?" asked the counselor.

"I have a job. We will manage," said Walt.

"What about it, Ms. Sherman?" she asked me.

As I continued to look at Walt, I thought, *Is he real? Does he really want to marry me and take on this tremendous responsibility?* "Are you sure, Walt?" I asked in a near-inaudible voice.

"Yes!" exclaimed Walt.

"Then okay," I said in a lighter voice.

"Well, if you're sure, Ms. Sherman, good luck. You'll need it." She seemed relieved and a bit happy for us.

As we walked out of the seemingly dark and cold clinic into the warm sunshine, Walt picked me up and swung me around. "We're going to have a baby!" he exclaimed. "I love you!" Then he kissed me. Oh, how I loved him at that moment! He could have left me and the baby. This wasn't going to be easy for him, yet he just proved his love! Truly, I was blessed in more ways than one but just didn't realize it then.

Now came the hard part—telling our parents. What made it even harder was that my dad wasn't home much since he was already working in Northern California. He came home only on the weekends, and then he and Mom were busy all the time. I became so frustrated!

I had told my sisters Cathy and Barbara. Cathy was married at that time. She had eloped to Las Vegas in May and called home to tell our parents. I'll never forget that day.

Mom had answered the phone, and I was just walking out the door. Barbara was there, and suddenly, I heard Mom cry out, "No!" Then she just slid to the floor, crying.

"What's wrong, Mom?" called out Barbara.

"No!" Mom moaned.

"What? What is it?" we both asked as we looked on the crumbled figure of our mother. She had her head buried in her knees while barely holding on to the phone. Barbara grabbed the phone. I asked Mom again, "What is it, Mom?"

"Cathy's married! She eloped!" cried Mom.

This was a very difficult time for everyone. How we got through it is one of God's mercies, yet none of us were aware of that at the time. The family having to move because of Dad's new job and having to leave Cathy behind was very hard for my parents. Now I was going to make it even more difficult, but there was nothing else I could do.

Walt and I tried to get my parents together to tell them, but it wasn't happening. One Friday evening, as I babysat my younger brothers and sisters while Mom and Dad went out with their best friends Frank and Iris, Walt, who was babysitting with me, said, "Let's tell them when they come home." We had to because the next time Dad came home, the family was moving up to Northern California.

When we heard the car drive up, we grabbed each other's hand and held tight. We heard Mom and Dad talking as they entered through the front door and turned into the kitchen. Slowly, we got up off the couch. As we came into the kitchen, I called out, "Mom! Dad! Dad, where's Mom?"

"She went to Iris's. Why?"

Not again! I thought. "Oh, nothing," was all I said. Then we went back into the living room and sunk back into the couch.

"Forget it!" I shouted under my breath.

"We can't forget it!" Walt said.

"I'm done trying to get them together! It's never going to happen!" I cried.

Walt patiently said, "We'll tell them tomorrow, all right?"

"Well, it better be tomorrow. Dad leaves Sunday, and the next time he comes home, we're moving!" I said as tears fell from my eyes.

Walt reassuringly said, "No matter what, we'll tell them tomorrow. I'd better head home for now. Don't cry! It'll be all right. Just go to bed and get some sleep. I'll see you as soon as I can tomorrow, okay?" He held me in his arms.

"Okay. I'll call you when it's all right to come over. I love you, babe. Will you always love me?" I asked.

"Yes! Of course I will! I will always love you," he said and kissed me good night.

"You better head on home, Walt," Dad said as we walked into the kitchen.

"Good night, Mr. Sherman," said Walt, and he left. Needless to say, I didn't sleep much that night, and neither did Walt.

As I went to bed, Barbara, who had came in earlier and had gone to bed, asked, "Well, did you guys tell them?"

"No! Mom went to Iris's, and we didn't get a chance!" I said, and then I cried.

"Well, you better do it tomorrow. Dad leaves soon, and then there won't be any more time. You have to tell them while Dad's here. Mom won't be able to handle it," Barbara said.

"I know! I know! We're trying! What am I going to do if I can't get them together?"

"You just have to do it tomorrow no matter what, okay?" Barbara said, trying to calm me.

"Sure, if I can. I'll do my best." Then I fell into a fretful sleep.

The next day, I called Walt as soon as everyone was up. It was around 9:30, so I figured there was time. Cathy and her husband, Mark, came over, and Mom and Dad had left for the grocery store. Walt showed up at that time, and I let him in and chased the younger siblings out to play, then we all went into the living room.

Cathy asked how it went.

"It didn't!" I exclaimed.

"What? You've got to be kidding!" laughed Cathy. "Patty, you can't put it off any longer. Dad leaves tomorrow! You have to tell them today!"

"No kidding!" I cried out. "We've tried, but every time we go to tell them, one of them leaves or they tell us, 'Not now!' It's so frustrating! What am I going to do?"

"Well, for starters, you have to tell them when they get back. Be sure to tell them together and in this way, 'Mom, Dad, I'm going to have a baby.' That way, they'll think of a grandbaby and will be happy, sort of. Then I'll tell them I'm going to have a baby too!" Cathy said with a smile.

"No! Really? When did you find out?" we all asked.

"Just recently," said Cathy.

"Oh how wonderful! We'll be pregnant together," I said. What Barbara was thinking, I don't know. She was pretty quiet through it all.

Finally, after what seemed like forever, Mom and Dad returned home. Walt and I got up, and everyone whispered, "Get in there!"

"I'm scared!" I cried under my breath.

"Don't be," whispered Cathy. "Just remember to say you're going to have a baby."

"I'm going to ask your dad if I can marry you," exclaimed Walt quietly.

"Yeah! That's what you should do," said Barbara and Cathy in a hushed assuring way. "Now go do it!"

Just then, we heard Mom say, "I've had it! I'm tired!"

"Well, why don't you go to Iris's and the kids and I will put the groceries away," said Dad. We hurried in to stop her.

"Mom, wait! I want to talk to you," I said.

"Not now! I'm going to Iris's!"

"But..." And she was gone.

I turned and went back into the living room. "See?" I said emphatically yet quietly! "It's never going to happen! Now Mom's gone!" I exclaimed under my breath.

"Patty, you guys get back in there and tell Dad then. It must be done now!" ordered Cathy. "Just remember to say you're having a baby. Dad has always wanted to be a grandpa, and this will help him see that. Now get in there!"

"But what about Mom?" I asked.

"Just tell Dad, and he'll help you tell Mom," said Cathy.

Walt and I walked into the kitchen then, and I quietly said, "Dad, I need to talk with you."

"Not now, Patty. I have the groceries to put away. You can help me."

"No, Dad! I need to talk with you," I said.

"Not now, Patty. Help me get the groceries put away before everything melts," he answered me.

"Dad! We need to talk *now!*" I exclaimed eagerly as tears filled my eyes, but I fought them back, then I went on. "We really need to talk to you and Mom, but you guys will never listen! Now Mom's gone, and you won't listen to me again!" I cried out loudly.

"What? What are you talking about?" he asked.

Finally, I had his attention. "Dad," I went on, "I need to tell you something important, so please sit down." Walt and I slid behind the table and sunk into two chairs across from where my dad had slowly sat down.

"All right. What's up?" he asked with a bit of a bewildered but staunch look.

Walt nervously spoke up then and said, "Well, Mr. Sherman, I'd like to ask you if I could marry Patty." A pause came, and then slowly, Dad looked at me and asked, "Why?"

"Well, Dad, I'm going to have a baby," I gingerly stated. A thick silence filled the room. It was so thick you could slice it.

Finally, I spoke up with a choked voice, "We've been trying to tell you and Mom, but you won't ever stop and let us. Whenever we tried to tell you together, one of you left! Just like Mom did now!" I explained to Dad. He looked in my eyes and saw the fear, and then he looked at Walt. He was summing the situation up, I could tell, and Walt too. Was that a smile I detected briefly on his face?

"We will have to discuss this with your mother when she gets back."

"We've tried to get you two together. Now Mom's at Iris's again!" I cried.

"Well, we are just going to wait until she gets back," said Dad.

Just then, as Walt and I arose from our chairs and headed toward the living room to wait once again, Mom walked in.

"I forgot my cigarettes," she stated.

Dad looked at me and gave a nod of his head. I took a deep breath and started, "Mom, I need to talk to you."

"Not now! I'm going to Iris's!" I tore up once again and looked longingly into my Dad's eyes.

"Mary Ann, you better stay."

"NO! I need a break! I'm going!"

"No, Mary Ann. You'd better sit down. Patty has something she wants to tell you," said Dad as he looked intently into Mom's eyes.

Mom then looked up to Dad and, with a sense of fear, said, "Russ?"

Dad's gaze then turned gentle as he looked into her eyes, which were filled with anxiety, and said again, "Sit down, honey.

Patty needs to talk with you." Mom then turned her anxious eyes to me.

"Mom, I'm going to have a baby," I said.

"Walt wants to marry her," stated my dad.

"No!" gasped Mom as she fell into the nearest chair. "Not again!" she said in a wisp of a voice. She started to cry lightly. "She's too young, Russ! She can't…We can't…" She stumbled as her mind spun.

Then Dad gently interrupted and said, "Mary Ann, let's go into the other room to talk." They told us to wait in the living room. Then Dad gently led Mom into the master bedroom, which once was theirs. They had given it up so Barbara and I could have it. They had given so much for their children, and now they were about to decide if they were going to have to give their daughter up too.

"Well? How did it go?" asked everyone.

"They went into the bedroom to talk. I don't know what they'll say. No matter what, I want to marry you, Walt!" I exclaimed under my breath. "I'll run away if I have to. I won't move!" I was so frightened. So was Walt.

"Do you think they'll not let you marry me?" he asked anxiously.

"I don't know, but I'll marry you one way or another!" I so arrogantly exclaimed.

"Oh, don't worry. Dad will help Mom to see what's best," stated Cathy.

"Yeah, maybe we better start putting the groceries away," said Barbara. I'm sure Barbara sensed just how heavy this was for our parents, and she wanted to help in any way she could.

"Yeah," agreed Cathy. "They won't be in the mood to deal with this mountain of groceries." So we all walked out to the kitchen and finished putting the mounds of groceries away while hardly speaking a word to each other.

CHAPTER 3

It seemed like an eternity, but finally, my parents submerged from the room. I could see that Mom was completely upset and saddened. Her eyes were swollen and red. She took my hand and led me into the front bedroom. I was a bit nervous as it usually meant a stern spanking when this happened. Yet, Mom's grasp was gentle, and as she closed the door, I saw a deep love and concern in her eyes, but they were glazed over in pain.

"Patty," she said, "you know, your father and I could arrest Walt for statutory rape." I was so ready to scream that they couldn't do that! I'm sure my face told that I was completely upset by that news. Mom then continued, "But your father and I have decided to let you get married. Your father said if it was anyone else other than Walt, the answer would be no. I think you're too young, but Dad said to let you get married." The tenderness was now gone, and a sterner look came over Mom.

I then said, "If it was anyone other than Walt, I wouldn't be in this condition. I love him, like I tried to tell you before, and I want to marry him, and he wants to marry me."

"It's not like playing with dolls, you know, Patty," stated Mom.

"I know, Mom! We love each other and want to have this baby!"

"Well, you can have this baby, and your father and I can raise it, and you can continue with school and growing up. You don't have to get married."

You could have knocked me over with a feather! In my mind, I was screaming, *No! I would never let you raise my child!* What arrogance I had! What disrespect! My dear mother was only try-ing to help me out of a very difficult situation in the only way her mother's heart could think of. It didn't take me long to respond to her suggestion though.

"No, Mom!" I exclaimed. "We'll raise this baby. I'll stay in school and finish it. Walt will continue to work. We've already thought this through."

Mom then looked in my eyes and a bit disgustingly said, "Obviously, you guys weren't thinking!" Mom and I never did have a good relationship. I didn't respect or understand her, and she didn't respect or understand me.

Right after speaking with my parents, my father said we needed to go tell Walt's parents. He asked if we wanted them to come. Walt said no, that it would probably be best if we just went. I was so glad because, as usual, I was upset at my mother and what she had said and just wanted to leave.

On the way over, as Walt was driving, we discussed what my parents had said. Walt was surprised about my mom offering to raise the baby. He was glad that I told her no and chose to marry him. I reminded him that I had chosen that before we talked to my parents. Then I asked how he felt his parents would react. "Oh, they will be okay with it. Anyways, I'm eighteen and don't need their approval." It wasn't as easy as Walt thought.

"Walt!" exclaimed his mother as she sunk down into a chair. "No!"

"So you've decided to get married?" gently asked his father.

"Yes," Walt stated. "We've already talked to Patty's parents, and they said we could."

"So they're all right with you getting married? I thought that your family's moving up north," his father questioned.

"They still are," I said sadly.

"Well, I guess we're all right with you getting married," Mr. Meyer said, and it was settled. "But when and where will you guys get married?" We hadn't thought about that. Well, actually I had.

My mom's best friend, Iris, had a daughter who became pregnant out of wedlock, and they had a beautiful wedding and reception, so I figured that the same thing would happen for me! Was I ever wrong!

The very next day, my father had to go back to Northern California. The burden of getting me married was placed square on my mother's shoulders for my family was moving in a few weeks! Mom turned to Iris for help. I don't know all that they discussed but I didn't get the wedding I was hoping for.

First, Mom took Walter and I to see our priest. She explained why we were there and that we had hoped to get married in the church. The priest asked if Walt was a Catholic.

"No," stated Mom.

"Well, that posses a problem," stated the priest. "Would he be willing to become Catholic?"

"I don't know," was all I said. I looked at Walt and he shrugged his shoulders.

"There's another problem, Father," injected Mom. "We are moving, her father and I, in a few weeks. That's not enough time to get her marriage license. They need a blood test, and it is a six-to-eight-week waiting period."

"Well, with her already expecting and you going to move," he said, "I think it would be best if they get married in Las Vegas. If they're still married in three years, we can marry them in the church. That way, if they end up in divorce, the church wouldn't have sanctioned it. We could annul the marriage, and she could still be married in the church. If they are still married after three years, they could say their vows in the church, and their marriage would then be sanctioned by the church."

I was furious! What was he thinking? Divorce before we were even married? Never! We'd show the church and everyone else! Mom, on the other hand, thought it was a good idea. I sensed relief come over her. As we left, I told her we would never divorce.

"How do you know, Patty? It isn't as easy as you think!" she said.

"I know we won't! Especially after what he said!" I said in a raised voice.

"Hush! You won't talk that way about Father! He knows more than you do! Now let's go! I have to call your dad," was all she had to say on the matter.

We told my parents on Saturday, November 9, 1974, and we were married on Tuesday, November 12, 1974. During those few days, Walt took me to Kmart to buy wedding rings. Mom offered to pay for Walt's, but he said he wanted to buy them both. They were simple gold bands, with diamond shaped etchings and didn't cost much, but it was more than he could afford.

Looking back, my poor parents must have been going through such a difficult time. My mother wanted to do her best by me, and my dad wished to be there for me and my mother but could not. Walt's parents too as this had happened to them once before and they had higher hopes for their son. Nonetheless, our parents stood by us the best they knew how. Now I can see God's hand in it all.

Our mothers were the only ones to go with us. My father couldn't even give me away, and that was hard for all involved. I had to borrow a skirt outfit, slip, and shoes from my sister Cathy. Mom suggested I wear the dress she had bought me for the prom, but I wanted something new. After all, it was my wedding. I figured if Mom saw me with my sister's borrowed clothes, that she would buy me something new. Was I wrong! It never happened.

When we arrived in Las Vegas, we went to a store, and I hoped Mom would at least buy me a pair of shoes. When I asked her to, she pointed to a pair of silver rolled-up flats! *Really!* I thought. *How ugly!* So I had nothing new to wear. We went to the courthouse, and Mom had to sign permission for me to get married since I was underage. Walt then signed his part, and we were told to head to the judge's chambers.

First, I had to change since I wore jeans for the long trip, so we headed to the ladies' room. It was your typical public restroom—

no pretty pictures or flowers, just drab-tiled floors and brown stalls. As I was in a stall trying to get on my nylons, my foot slipped into the commode! There was a little girl in the next stall, and she heard the commotion.

"Mommy," she asked, "is that lady okay?"

The mom knew why I was there as she had seen us in the lobby. "I think so, honey," she said as she giggled lightly.

Just then, Mom came into the restroom and hollered out, "Patty! What's taking you so long?"

I started to silently cry. This was not what I had hoped for. I hurried as quickly as my heavy heart would let me. All Mom could do was rush me. All I wanted from her at that moment was a reassuring hug, but it never came.

Finally, I gathered myself together and put my head up and walked out to meet my future husband, the man I loved more than words could say. He could see that I had been crying, and he came over and put his arm around me and whispered, "It's going to be okay, honey. I love you." Then off we went to the judge's chambers.

The room was just a small office with three chairs and a desk in the corner. The judge asked if we were ready, and we said we were. He then asked who would witness our union, and our moms said they would.

"Fine," he said. "Then I'll have the young couple stand here in front of my desk, and I'll have you, Mrs. Meyer, stand next to your son, and you, Mrs. Sherman, stand next to your daughter." We took our places, and the judge looked at us and smiled reassuringly then began.

I shall never forget the atmosphere as we said our vows. As we repeated those sacred vows, it seemed as if everyone else disappeared from view. Then a cloud came down and surrounded us. I sensed God's presence. Even though I had never experienced it before, I knew that it was God. He came and was sealing this holy union. I was literally awed by it. This picture would help me hold true to my marriage through many difficult situations. Then as we sealed our vows with the exchange of the rings and a kiss, we began our life as husband and wife.

CHAPTER 4

We had no place to move in to and no money to do it with either. That being the case, we had to live with my parents for the first two weeks while they prepared to move. They had sold the house before we had told them of our situation. Later, my mom would tell me she wished we would have told her sooner. That way, they would have rented us the four-bedroom house for the payment of $147. That would have been great, but God knew, and that wasn't in his plans for any of us.

Walt's parents lived in a two-bedroom house, and Walt's brother, Bill, was occupying one of the bedrooms, his parents the other and their grandchild; whom they had guardianship of; was sleeping on the hide-a-bed, so it wasn't possible to move in with them. It seemed more doable to move in with my parents even though this was difficult for my whole family, but Mom really wanted us to.

There were seven others living in that house at the time. My father was up north, and my sister Cathy was living in her own apartment with her husband, Mark, but there were my six other siblings, Mom, and now Walt and me.

The house was a four-bedroom ranch. It had a living room, two bathrooms, and a large eat-in kitchen. The eat-in area was large enough for two tables. One was able to sit eight, and a smaller one sat six.

My three brothers—Joe, Kenny, and Jerry—were sharing a bedroom; my two younger sisters—Susie and Annie—were sharing a bedroom; and now my older sister Barbara had to move out of the bedroom we had shared for years and sleep in the bedroom Cathy had slept in. Mom and Dad had given Barbara and me the master bedroom, which had its own bathroom, a while back. Now Walt and I had this room. Mom was sleeping on the couch as that was where Mom and Dad had been sleeping for quite some time.

During our stay there, I was oblivious to what everyone else was going through. My brothers and sisters were having to say good-bye to their lifelong friends. Barbara had just graduated the same time Walt had and was now having to move to a new area along with having to determine her college plans. Dad was gone trying to locate a home for his ever-shrinking-yet-large family. And Mom, well, Mom was still trying to help me get settled as much as she could before she had to move and leave me and Cathy behind. I just realize now how difficult this had to be for her. I was so self-centered and immature at the time that I couldn't see beyond me.

She brought me to my high school and to the vice-principal's office. I felt it ironic that I was going to the principal's office, as if I was in trouble. Yet, wasn't I? My mother understood too plainly that I was indeed in trouble and needed help.

We sat in front of the vice-principal's desk as my mother poured out her concerns of wanting me to continue school. Mr. Nelson, the vice-principal, then called in the girls' assistant principal, Mrs. Bernstein. He filled her in to my predicament and asked for any suggestions.

The schools back then, although changing, had not yet allowed pregnant girls to remain on campus. They felt it was too much of a distraction and would have a negative impact on their students. (I agreed and feel it should still be that way.) Mom understood but asked if there was any way I could remain in school.

The two of them talked briefly and told us that they did have a program for pregnant students. It was off campus, so it would not interfere with regular school life. Ms. Judeivine, the teacher, was a talented educator dedicated to helping girls in my situation not only finish school but also prepare for motherhood. This was such a relief for Mom to hear. That's what she was so concerned about—not just me finishing school, but she wouldn't be here to help me with my newborn baby.

I didn't see it that way though. I was frightened. Frightened of what my unknown future held but also saddened because my family was moving. It seemed to me that Mom was just trying to push me out and that Dad didn't even care. After all, he wasn't even at my "wedding," and now he wouldn't even come home to help me!

I was also determined to show Mom I was more than capable of handling things. Little did I know just how incapable I was. I felt like telling her I'd handle it. Really? How? I was so stupid and arrogant! Thank God that he gave me such a strong mother and father. They knew me well and guided me, even when I was so much of a trial to them. Thank God they never gave up on me.

We made an appointment to meet Ms. Judeivine and have her explain the curriculum. We met her at the Baptist church located just around the block from my parents' house. The young mothers' class met in the hall of the church. She gave us a short tour of the building. As we came to the kitchen, she pointed out that we would be learning cooking, shopping, and even some interior decorating. I was quite excited about that!

Ms. Judeivine assured my mother that my schooling would not diminish. She reassured her that I would be learning all the needed courses to pass eleventh grade and also some life skills. Besides what she had already mentioned, we'd be learning budgeting, shopping, and care of the baby. This was such a blessing! Not only did it help Mom to be relieved, but I was truly looking forward to it. I never wanted to quit school, but my child would always come first. This way, I was able to accomplish both goals. So I enrolled in the young mothers' class of Bonita High.

Shortly after our marriage, Walt's parents received the sad news that his grandpa Meyer had died suddenly, so they had

PATRICIA MEYER

to leave for Illinois for the funeral. It saddened them further to know that Walt would not be able to go with them.

We moved into their house while they were away. This gave my parents time without us in the way to pack and prepare to move. Dad had returned home, and now Mom could rely on his strength. These were difficult times for all of us in more ways than one.

By the time Mom and Pop Meyer, as I started to call them, arrived home, my parents had moved to Petaluma, California. We lived with Walt's parents for a couple more weeks, and then they helped us get into a one-bedroom apartment in the same town, La Verne.

The apartment was one of four in a building complex of six such buildings. As you walk into our apartment, you'd walk right into the living room. It was a very nice size. Just off to the right was the eat-in kitchen—your standard-sized apartment kitchen, with one side of cupboards with room for a refrigerator, a stove at the end, and a sink on the other wall set in a cupboard. Then there was room for a small table-and-chair set. We had to supply the appliances, which were given to us—a normal stove and a refrigerator, which was an old one with a foot-square freezer! It was old but big enough for us, and we were grateful.

As a matter of fact, all of our furniture was used and given to us by family and friends. Later, even the crib and baby dresser would be. The crib was found in our friends' garage, which was in our apartment complex, and the antique dresser was found in an auto junkyard warehouse that was run by one of Walt's friends.

Walt was working where he had been since he was sixteen, at Hagen-& Renaker in San Dimas. He was making $2 an hour and working all day. Our rent was $130 a month, and it was all we could do to make it from paycheck to paycheck.

I was still trying to be the cool high school kid, so soon after we moved into our apartment, I told my school friends to pass the word that we were going to have a party. It was a "bring your own beer" party, so I didn't think Walt would mind.

He did mind. "You're pregnant, and I'm tired after working all day, honey! Why did you do that?" he asked me.

"I just want to party with everyone! After all, we have our own place now, so why not?" I stubbornly asked. This was the beginning of Walt having to deal with an immature wife, and although he was capable, it was something he hadn't bargained on.

We had the party, and we had people coming out of the woodwork! Needless to say, the party ended up with cops and trouble. There was mayhem as kids scattered in all directions. Thankfully, as the police realized the unique situation Walt was in as they looked at my large belly, they had mercy. They could have arrested him since he was a legal adult and there were minors involved, but they let us go after they gave Walt a clear warning, and then they cleared the crowd that had hung around. You'd think this would be lesson enough, but it didn't stop the partying, even after the baby arrived.

I had just turned seventeen and Walt nineteen, both in March of 1975. It was seven in the morning on May 30, 1975, and the beginning of quite an eventful time. It was the day of the arrival of our beautiful daughter, June Ann Meyer. A day we will always cherish. This little bundle of joy was why we changed our plans. She was what made it all worthwhile. It wasn't easy, but we were so blessed! Even though neither of us knew the Lord, we knew that June was truly a gift from heaven.

The one difficult situation at that time was that neither of my parents could be there. It was sad not to have Mom there at least. I cried to Walt about it, and he just reassured me they would be if they could. My mom had her best friend, Iris Herman, be there in her place. I was grateful as Iris added the motherly comfort I needed, yet she wouldn't be able to be there until after the birth of June Ann.

Some of the nurses treated me quite badly during the labor. One even said I was too young to know what I was feeling as she left the room right after I told her I thought the baby was about to be delivered. Thank God Walt entered the room just then.

"Honey, I love you!" he anxiously said as he walked over to the bedside.

"Where were you?" I questioned as I fought through another labor pain.

"They took me to fill out papers! I'm sorry, honey," he said as he stroked my hair. I told him how the nurse had treated me, and he reassured me it would be fine and that we were going to be good parents. Tears started to fill my eyes, but then suddenly, I was jolted to the urgent plight of my delivery!

"The baby's coming, Walt! Do something! Get someone!" I said as I fought through another intense labor pain less than a minute later. So he ran to get the nurse, and within thirty minutes, June arrived!

We had chosen her name before she was born, and as I held her in my arms later that day, it didn't matter what the nurse had said. It didn't matter what anyone thought of me. It only mattered what this little girl would think of me. I hoped to be the best mommy she could ever have. She was so precious and innocent! She only deserved the very best! I cried as I felt my heart fill with love unspeakable for this beautiful baby God had just given me. I knew Walt was feeling those same emotions as he came up to me and, with tears in his eyes, said, "I love you! She's so beautiful. Look at her!" Then they took him out to the waiting room while they prepared the baby and me for transferring us to our rooms. Mine was a hospital room, and June's was the nursery.

I was placed in a room with four other young mothers. I think one of them was married but not all. We were situated out of the main stream of new mothers. It was quite obvious we were not respected by most of the staff, and this made our special time a very sad experience. I was thankful that Iris came later that day.

"Your mom would be here, you know, Patty, if she could. I know you must miss her," Iris stated.

"Oh, I do! I wish she could have come down," I sadly said.

"You know that, that wasn't possible, Patty. They haven't enough money to pay for a ticket. If it was at all possible, your mom at least would be here. After all, this is her first grandchild," she told me with a big smile.

"I know that. Thanks for coming and seeing me," I said once again, sadly.

"I would've came anyways, honey," she stated. "Your baby is so cute! What's her name?"

"June Ann," I responded.

"That's a pretty name," she said. "You know, you're quite a lucky girl! You have a beautiful little daughter, and Walt's a great guy. I'm sure he'll make a wonderful father."

"I know he will," I replied.

"And you'll make a great mother," she gently stated.

Finally, the cloud that was hanging over my head because my parents weren't there lifted. I looked up into Iris's smiling face and smiled back. "Yeah!" I said quietly. "I will." With that, Iris said good-bye. I will forever be grateful for that dear woman and my mother's love to have sent her best representation to my side.

In celebration of the birth of our babies, the hospital offered us a dinner of steak, baked potato, vegetable, and choice of dessert to be eaten with your husband or companion. This is how I came to realize that not all the girls were married, or even had their boyfriend still.

As they came in to deliver the meals, Walt was there and another guy, but that was it. We all drew our curtains to have some privacy, and I could hear someone crying softly as we ate. I felt sorry for her and realized just how lucky I was that Walt had stayed with me. I felt love for him that I hadn't felt before at that moment. A love of respect and admiration. This was a good love, but one that would be tested in the months ahead.

As time went on, I would feel alone because Walt was working all day and then come home too tired to do anything. We had absolutely no extra money and never seemed to make ends meet without going to Walt's parents every weekend to do laundry and eat. I was so depressed that I had even attempted suicide.

On this bleak day, I had lost hope and was overly tired because the baby would not stop crying. I became highly aware that I was not fit to be a mother. I felt like no one cared if I died and June would be better off without me. So I wrote a note stating such and proceeded to down a whole bottle of Acetaminophen.

My plan was simple. I would take the pills shortly before Walt was due home. That way he would be home before anything could happen to June when I died. She was such a tiny baby still.

"Ninety nine, one hundred," I continued to count as I took the pills. "I just can't go on!" I cried as I proceeded to swallow the last pill. "No one will really care. June and Walt are better off without me. Mom! I wish you were here, but you never listened to me anyways." I was such a pitiful, self-centered, immature little girl, but that was the problem! I did have enough sense to put June in her baby bed before I blacked out. Walt came home and found me knocked out and June crying in her crib.

Exactly what happened is a blur to me, but I do know that Walt must have taken care of June and then came to my rescue once again. I remember him cooking and feeding me. I remember throwing up and him telling me that, that was good. I was so young and stupid! So ungrateful and, as I now realize, so very scared! Walt, on the other hand, was taking on the role of provider, husband, and father so completely, yet I am sure he was just as overwhelmed as me, if not more!

We pulled through that dreadful day and moved on with our lives. We found our only happiness in our daughter. To see her grow and have such childish joy was the only light in our ever-darkening world.

As she grew and quickly advanced, she learned to pull herself up in the cradle. The time came when June needed to be placed in a crib and she needed her own dresser. That's when we were lucky enough to find both and didn't have to pay a dime for either.

The crib was white with a blue teddy bear and a pink lamb, one on both ends. The dresser was brown, and I was so hoping to have a matching set. Walt figured we could paint the dresser white to help it match a bit. I then thought that maybe we could find some Winnie the Pooh stickers and place them on it as I had saved up blue chip stamps and got a Winnie the Pooh toy chest for June. Walt suggested we look in the local five-and-ten store to see if we could find any stickers that would work.

We went immediately to the local store. As I kept looking for Winnie the Pooh, I realized we wouldn't be able to afford the icon stickers. Walt kept digging as he saw my disappointment. He suddenly stopped and with wide eyes and a big grin on his face, exclaimed, "Look!"

As he pulled the sheets of stickers out of the drawer, I could slightly make out blue teddy bears and pink lambs. "These will match the crib!" he joyfully stated.

I went over and childishly whined, "But they're not Winnie the Pooh!"

"Honey, they match perfectly," Walt patiently stated.

"Yeah, but I wanted Winnie the Pooh," I said, a bit more subdued. I realized we wouldn't be able to afford the icon stickers, but I was trying to force my way.

Walt was ever so patient with me. He truly did want to give me anything I wanted but knew it was not possible. "Honey, I promise I'll do a good job of painting the dresser, and you'll see that these will work. We can't afford the other stickers. It'll look great. Let's just take them home, and after I paint the dresser, we can hold them up, and you can decide then."

So we took them home, and they worked perfectly. Now our little baby could have a beautiful crib and dresser that matched with the cutest little figures on it. It makes my heart warm even now to remember it. I was unable to see the hand of God in even this small detail of our life then, but this was only one of many ways God took care of us.

We celebrated our second Christmas with all the trimmings thanks to our dear friends Iris and Frank setting us up with a huge free Christmas tree and all the makings of a Christmas dinner, all complements of the local Boys Scout troop. My sister

Cathy gave us a wooden set of decoupage ornaments Walt and I could put together, and Walt's parents gave us some lights.

We were able to buy a couple of toys from the local bargain store, and I was given a pretty red dress for June. It was a happy time for us all. Having June in our lives was the only joy we experienced, and we were both so much in love with her. Yet our love for each other seemed to dwindle.

Our lives just went down from there, like it could go any further! In June of 1976, Walt decided we needed to move to the two-bedroom apartment next door as our neighbor lady had just told us she was moving out. We thought having more room would help. It did for a bit.

The move was the worst move I ever made! Everything was just brought into the living room and dumped for me to wade my way through. Walt and I finally got the place in order. I had told Walt that I wish we could do something with the place to make it more ours. So he went to the manager and asked if we could put wallpaper and paint. We were given permission and excitedly went to the store to pick out paint and paper. We were able to do this with the tax return money we had received.

The wallpaper had a brown lattice work on it with orange-and-yellow flowers with some greenery woven in. We painted the walls a light yellow and bought some kitchen curtains to match. I told Walt I wished we had a room divider to separate the kitchen from the living room, and as always, he did what he could to make it happen.

He proceeded to build us a portable bar out of used lumber. I thought it was wonderful! It had rope in between the boards that formed the top counter. It had shelves with front doors, made of amber colored Plexiglas framed in the wood, that would face the living room, the opened back would face the dining area and it was framed with an overhead place for lighting. Then he stained it and slightly burned it and finished it with a heavy varnish. It looked to me as if it could have been in a beach house. Just what I wanted!

Walt was so good to me, always finding ways to make me happy. Our happiness was temporary, though, as the months went on.

We fought constantly, always over money and the lack thereof. Walt never wanted to hit me, but I was always angry and shouting at him! He was getting drunk more and more, and at times, we fought physically. I was even drinking more.

We continued to party, hoping to find relief from our responsibilities. We would party with our drinking friends, and even had our little baby, June Ann, with us as we did. We thought we were being such good parents by keeping her with us.

She was by my side always. I never once thought of the danger we were placing her in until one night when I got so drunk and I could barely remember stumbling home. Thankfully, Walt wasn't quite as drunk as me, and we got home without much incident. This made us realize something had to change. We felt trapped in our current situations but didn't know what we could do to change them.

Later that year, we drove nine hours up to Northern California to visit my parents for the New Year celebration of 1977, and while we were there, Walt checked where my brother Joe worked. He thought it was just an all-right job. It was factory work, and Walt hated factory work, but the pay was a lot more than Walt made, and it was a union job with benefits. As we drove home, we talked about where Joe worked and how great it would be if Walt made that kind of money at Hagen-Renaker.

It was now around June of the same year, and we had had many difficult situations happen in our short time of marriage, some which involved the police and jail. These were turbulent times for us.

I had started working at the local pizza parlor to help alleviate some pressure. It only caused more though, as Walt was very jealous. He hated that I was working amongst a bunch of guys my age and waiting on older men who drank. He had a right to be worried, but I just couldn't see it.

"I have to work, Walt!" I said once while we were arguing about it. "We can't make it on what you're making at Hagen and Renaker, and remember, you wanted me to!" As a matter of fact, his mother had once said while bailing Walt out of jail, "Patty, it's just too much for Walt. He works too hard. Maybe you should get a job."

"I would," I replied. "But Walt doesn't want me to." Later that month was when he finally told me to look for a job, and that's when I started at the pizza parlor.

So now here we were with Walt making $2.10 an hour, and I was earning $1.25 an hour. We just found out we were expecting our second child, and Walt didn't want me to work anymore, and neither did I.

"Well, what if I got a better-paying job?" he asked.

"That would be great!" I said. "Where?"

"I was thinking about asking Joe if they were hiring where he works. Not only is it better pay, but there's benefits too, so the baby would be covered."

We were on medical assistance from the state of California, and Walt hated that. If I quit, we would qualify for food stamps and financial assistance, but Walt didn't want to do that. He wanted to take care of his family, and I admired him for that.

So he applied for the job at Cal-Wood Doors. He was hired, and we moved shortly thereafter. I was so excited to be moving close to my family. Even Cathy had moved up to where my parents lived the year prior. I was also glad to move for I knew that something had to change. Life as it was could no longer be, or it would destroy us.

So we packed up our things and moved to the same town my parents lived in, Rohnert Park in Northern California. We were going to start fresh and have a better life. At least Walt felt that he would be able to better provide for us, and he did. I was just happy to be living near my family once again. This was going to work. It had to, or we would lose everything, June Ann included. Thankfully, it was while we lived in Rohnert Park, California, that I first started to seek the Lord.

CHAPTER 5

We had moved to Rohnert Park in September 1977—Walt, June, and myself with a baby on the way. We rented a mobile home in Green Acres Mobile Home Park. It was a green-and-white double-wide mobile home with a carport and small side yard. The home had two descent-sized bedrooms with a washer and dryer, which didn't work, but there was a Laundromat on the grounds. It also had two bathrooms—one off the hall and one in the master bedroom. There was a large kitchen with a separate dining area and a living room, and it even came with curtains and appliances! I thought this was like moving into a mansion after our apartment.

We had our own yard, even if it was only postage-stamp size. We had a park with swings for June and the new baby to play in, and it had a pool. Plus, I could take the kids for walks around the neighborhood without getting out on the busy streets.

Rohnert Park was a beautiful community. It had lush greenery everywhere. The grass was green, and there were flowers in planters all around the stores and down the median of nearly every street. We lived not too far from the Northern Pacific Shores, and there were farmlands, vineyards, and rolling hillsides all around. I was so excited! Not to mention, I was now close to my family! Mom and Dad lived just a few miles away, and Cathy was nearby too.

Walt started working with Cal-Wood Door Company right away. He worked in their factory building doors. Although he hated working in a factory, he did it to better provide for us. He was a hard worker and soon was producing more doors than any-one else. The bosses were so impressed by him. A while later, they promoted him to installing the doors. This was a bit easier for him to take, and he enjoyed it.

Walt's dissatisfaction with working in a factory didn't help his drinking problem. As a matter of fact, he now was going to the bar with some of the guys from work on payday. Once, and only once, did he spend nearly all his check at the bar. When he sobered up, he realized what he had done and promised never to do that again—a promise that he kept, yet the drinking continued.

Shortly after we moved in, our second daughter arrived. It was December 4, 1977. This time, my parents were there. My dad was so excited to be the one to babysit June while we went to the hospital. This was an eventful time as with our first pregnancy. I had had a quick delivery with June, and this was even quicker! When she was born, the doctor asked what we were going to name her.

"Walter," is what I said.

"Well, honey," said the doctor, "she's a girl!"

"I planned for a boy! I didn't pick a girl's name," was my immature reply.

"Honey, we need to pick a girl's name," replied Walt in a more grown-up attitude. "I picked Walter! You pick it out," I said.

He looked down on his beautiful little girl and said, "How about Mandy?"

I hesitated for a moment. "That sounds pretty. Okay. Mandy it is," I agreed.

"Amanda?" questioned the doctor.

"No," replied Walt. "Mandy, just Mandy," he said as he looked so lovingly on her. I was then handed my new little girl and as I looked down on her sweet little face, a wave of love filled my heart. I gently drew her close and kissed her.

"Mandy," I whispered. "Mandy."

"What about a middle name?" questioned the doctor again.

"You pick it out, honey," Walt said to me. "I picked the first name. Now you pick out her middle name."

So I looked on her precious face and thought for a minute. "Lyn," I said, thinking that sounded sweet with Mandy.

"Okay. Lynn, that's L-Y-N-N," stated the doctor.

"No," I said. "Lyn. L-Y-N." And so it was settled.

We now had two precious little girls to take care of, but I felt something missing still. I was so lucky to have my sister Cathy nearby. We would get together with our kids and talk. We both had two little ones, but she had a boy, Mark, who was close in age to June, and a girl, Lisa, who was exactly eleven months older than Mandy.

Once while visiting with Cathy over at Mom's, I said I wished I would have graduated. I had quit school in my senior year because June was getting sick. I felt I needed to be with her and stop taking her out in the cold to the sitters every morning just so I could finish school.

So as we sat at Mom's table discussing it, Mom suggested I start continuation school.

"Where is that?" I asked.

"They have one locally. The one your sister Susan is going to," stated Mom.

"But I have two kids! How could I go with them?"

"Isn't it over by my apartment, Mom?" Cathy asked.

"Yes, it is," answered Mom.

"Then I could watch the girls while you're in class, Patty," Cathy offered.

"Let's check it out and see if you can do it."

"Okay. I will!" I said with anticipation and a little fear.

I enrolled in August of 1978. I would put the girls in a stroller and push them the mile and a half to Cathy's apartment and then walk the couple of blocks to the school. Being it was a continuation school, there were high school students who were placed there because of some difficulties they encountered while on the high school campus. Most, if not all, of those difficulties were caused by the students themselves, such as I had created in my life. Yet glad to say, there weren't any expecting mothers.

I did well in all my courses. I didn't have to take a full course load since I had partially attended twelfth grade. I appreciated this opportunity to finish school, and I greatly appreciated the teacher.

He would use me as an inspiration to the class from time to time.

"Now class," he would start, "look at Ms. Meyer. She has two little children to take care of and still finds time to finish her homework. There's no excuse for you not to." I told Mom what he said, and she said, "I wouldn't be so proud, Patty. After all, you got pregnant before marriage, and that's nothing to be proud of."

As usual, Mom was not supportive of me, and she couldn't give me an encouraging word. *No, Mom*, I thought. *But I am accomplishing school while raising two kids, and I'm only nineteen!* But I never spoke it.

I was quite depressed about Mom's remark. I went to my teacher and told him I was going to quit. "No, Patty! You only have a bit more to finish. You can do this! Just stick with it. You'll graduate soon," he encouraged. So I continued with school. It was made easier as I had Cathy to visit after class.

We'd take the kids for walks and sometimes go to McDonald's. We'd each order one hamburger and fries to split between our kids. Then order ourselves a fish fillet sandwich and remove half the bun. As usual, I was dieting. Cathy was quite a help in this area for me as well. She was the more disciplined one. We would talk about life and all its difficulties we both faced.

Cathy's husband, Mark, had abandoned her and the kids again. I thought my life was hard, but it was nothing compared to hers. Yet she seemed at peace about it. She shared with me that she found life bearable because she found the Lord. She knew I was so dissatisfied with life, so she invited me to attend her church, Calvary Chapel, on Sunday. I told her I'd go. Why not? Nothing else seemed to be working in my life.

Walt didn't want me to go. "What's wrong with the Catholic church you're going to?" he angrily spoke.

"Nothing!" I said. "I just want to go and see what it's like. Besides, what do you care?"

"Who's going to watch the kids?" he asked.

"You!" I stated firmly. "They're your kids too, you know! It'll only be for an hour. It won't kill you! I'm going, and that's final!" I shouted.

So on Sunday, I went with Cathy a bit nervously. I wasn't sure what to expect, but I would soon find out.

Calvary Chapel was a huge church, but we were warmly greeted by everyone. As we entered the sanctuary, I looked up in amazement at how huge it was! It was an auditorium with balcony seating.

We sat up about midway of the first-floor seating, right in the middle isle. There was an opening prayer and then singing—songs I had never sung—some testimonies, and then the preacher, Brother Smith, came to the podium.

What exactly he preached, I don't quite remember. I do remember that during his sermon, I came to see that I was missing something in my life. That the dissatisfaction I felt was because of what I was missing. I remember that after his sermon, he asked if anyone wanted to be saved, to have their sins forgiven and their heart changed. I figured this must be what I was missing, so I raised my hand.

"There's one hand. Is there anyone else who wishes to be saved?" Brother Smith asked. No one else raised their hand. "Well," he went on, "we won't embarrass you and have you come down here by yourself to the altar to pray. Cathy, is this your friend?"

"My sister, Patty," she replied.

"Okay then. We'll pray collectively for Patty, then, Cathy, you can meet with my wife in the prayer room and pray with her there." So we all prayed, and I was led by Cathy to a room on the main floor.

While in the room, Sister Smith led me in the penitent's prayer. Then she asked me how I felt. "Good," was all I said.

"Well, following Jesus will be a new experience for you. Just read your Bible and he will guide you," she told me.

"And, Patty," Cathy said, "you'll have to submit to Walter, you know. You really need help in this, so we'll be praying for you."

Submit to Walt? I thought. *Just how do I do that?* So I asked. "The Bible teaches that we're to obey our husbands no matter what. To do whatever they tell us," Cathy explained.

"Even if he told me to steal?" I flippantly asked.

"Yes!" was all she said.

"I can't believe that!" I remarked.

"You have to! It's in God's Word!" she firmly stated.

"Now, Cathy, we don't expect her to learn everything all at once," stated Sister Smith. Then she said, "We will meet for prayer and Bible study, okay?"

"That sounds good," said Cathy. "When can we get together?"

Looking to me, Sister Smith asked, "When is it good for you, Patty?"

Whoa! was all I thought. Bible study? Prayer? I was raised Catholic and was taught that only the priest could read the Bible, that the common people could not understand it. "I don't know," I hesitantly said.

"Come on, Patty. It won't hurt you, and I think it'll help you," Cathy said.

What do I have to lose? I thought. "Okay. I really don't care when, just during the day when Walt's at work."

"Then let's meet Tuesday. Does that work for you, Cathy?" Sister Smith questioned.

"That's fine for me. We'll have the kids, so let's meet at my apartment at ten," offered Cathy.

"That sounds good to me," said Sister Smith. "How about you, Patty?"

"That sounds fine for me," I said, and so it was set.

I can't say I felt any different even though Cathy was sure I would. It was all a bit strange to me, but I knew I needed to change things in my life, or my marriage wasn't going to make it. So began my journey of finding that something, or rather that someone.

At the Bible study, we read some scriptures and discussed what they said. I don't remember any of it except that I spoke very little since I really didn't understand it.

Then it came time to pray. We were sitting around the table, and Sister Smith said that we'd each pray, and then she led. After she prayed, Cathy prayed, asking God to help me understand about submission and thanking him for saving me. Then it was my turn.

I felt a bit uncomfortable as I had never prayed like this before. Then as I started, a beautiful sight came to my mind. It was one of a yellow daisy bent down to the ground. As I began to pray, I recall that the flower started to raise its bent head.

"Lord," I was praying, "let me be like a flower, turning my head to you. Let me drink in your sunshine and grow. Amen." And I was finished.

"That was beautiful, Patty!" stated Cathy. I thought to myself, *That's how I feel!* I didn't know what it meant, but I knew a change had come into my life.

As I continued to try to do all I was being taught, I had some strange things happen. Things I didn't understand at the time but now realize that I was in the midst of a battle. A spiritual battle. Satan was not going to let me go easily, but Christ was fighting for my soul. I hadn't grasped all this. I truly didn't understand, but God is patient and merciful. He knew exactly what I needed to understand.

2
BATTLE OF GOOD AND EVIL

"And there was in their synagogue a man with an unclean
spirit; and he cried out, saying, Let us alone; what have
we to do with thee, thou Jesus of Nazareth? art thou
come to destroy us? I know thee who thou art, the Holy
One of God. And Jesus rebuked him, saying, Hold thy
peace, and come out of him."

—Mark 1:23–25

CHAPTER 1

I started to try to change. I obeyed Walt when he told me he didn't want me to go to Calvary Chapel.

"But why don't you want me to go?" I asked.

"I just don't. Why not continue going to the Catholic church?" he questioned me.

"Can't you be a Christian in the Catholic church?"

"Well, yes. I guess I can, but they don't believe in letting me read the Bible," I stated.

"You can still read it. They can't stop you. Just go there and be a Christian," he said.

So I went to the Catholic church. Cathy wasn't happy. She didn't understand why Walt didn't want me to attend her church. "Just go with me anyways. He will understand later," Cathy suggested.

"But what about submitting to him? You said I was to submit no matter what, and it's not like he's asking me to steal or something," I stated.

"You're right," she said. "Who knows? Maybe this will help Mom and Dad get saved. All right. But keep coming to prayer meeting and Bible study. Keep reading your Bible at home, and be a good witness in the church. Maybe you can teach catechism. That way, you might help someone understand the love of Christ."

So I did start helping and attending the Catholic church faithfully. I was being the best Christian Catholic I knew how to be. As I taught catechism, I began to see the discrepancies the Catholic religion had compared to the Bible. It concerned me, and I would ask Walt and my dad questions. Mostly though, I'd observe and ponder the questions in my heart.

Day after day, I tried and tried to be the good wife. Cathy reprimanded me for wasting my time planning my days around the television. She was right, and I started to take the girls for more walks, playtime in the park, and swimming. I also became a better housekeeper. My big sister knew me well, and I appreciated all she did to help me.

It seemed like a lifetime, but in actuality, it had only been a few months. It was now August 1978. I was really struggling with submission because Walt continued to drink, not that I felt like there was anything wrong with drinking at that time. I still partook in it occasionally myself. On the other hand, Walt drank to get drunk, and I was getting fed up with it.

One cool evening, Walt and my brother Joe and his friend Tim were drinking heavily. They had gone fishing that day and were just having a "good" time afterward. I had spent all day alone with the kids and was tired.

We had played at the park on the swings and had walked over to visit with Cathy. June and Mandy were happy and enjoyed the park and visiting with their cousins. I, on the other hand, was a very unhappy person, and I needed help.

"Walt makes me so mad!" I said.

"Now, Patty. He's your husband, and he just needs some free time after working hard all week. You're lucky that he's such a hard worker," Cathy said. I knew she was right, but it was difficult. I just couldn't stand him drunk, and he was drunk everyday!

Now looking back, I see that I was pretty self-centered. I at least had a husband who was willing to go to work to provide for us, and he came home every day; Cathy did not. Mark had deserted her and their kids once again, yet she helped me see that I had God to turn to and could go to him any time and he would help. She was right, and I went home.

On the walk home, I thought about it. I really had no relationship with God. I was just doing what Cathy helped me with. I tried to talk with God, but I never seemed to connect. Yet I knew something had happened to me at that service a couple months ago. Why then was I unable to really connect? I didn't know, but I kept trying anyway. I prayed that God would help me and that he would change Walt. I felt that if he didn't change, I would just leave with the girls.

When I got home, the guys were there, and we decided to barbecue. After we ate, I gave June and Mandy their baths. I enjoyed this because they were so cute! They were my reason for living. They needed me, and I needed them. They needed their father too, but it seemed he never had enough time for them or me. Thinking of this made anger grow inside me.

When the girls' baths were finished, I dressed them in their pajamas. I took them into their bedroom and read them a short story and said prayers with them, something I had just started. After tucking them in and giving them a good-night kiss on their cheeks, I went out to the living room where the guys were.

I couldn't stand their drunkenness, so I headed into the kitchen. I needed to clean up anyway. As I washed the dishes, I tried to pray, but instead, my thoughts turned to my unhappy life. The guys just got louder and louder. They had turned on the stereo and had the music blasting.

I went in to check on the girls, and they were stirring. I went and turned the music down some. "The kids are trying to sleep," was all I said. I went back into the kitchen to finish up and got myself a drink of diet soda.

The music was turned up again. I stomped back into the living room and turned it back down. "The kids are trying to go to sleep, you idiot!" I shouted at Walt.

"It's my house too, and I'll listen to the music how I want to," he slurred as he proceeded to turn up the music once again.

"No, you're not!" I shouted as I turned the music off. "The kids need to sleep, and they can't with these panel walls and that music blasting! It's keeping them awake, and it's their bedtime!" I continued to shout, as if that wouldn't keep them awake.

Well, this went on for a bit until Joe convinced Walt that it didn't have to be quite that loud. I went back and checked on the girls. "You kids go to sleep. It's okay. Just go to sleep." I told June and Mandy as they looked up at me with big questioning eyes. They, like any other child would, showed fear when we fought. After reassuring them, I went back into the living room.

"I'm going to bed," I tartly said.

"Uh-oh. Maybe we should go," suggested Tim.

"Nah! Stay! It's not late," said Walt. I turned sharply and headed for the bedroom.

After I changed into my nightie, I lay down on the bed and fumed. I tried praying, but I was just too angry because Walt turned up the stereo once again. Then he turned it up again, and now it really was too loud.

As the music blasted through the house, I stormed out of my bedroom, still in my nightie, fuming mad. I bent down and briskly turned the stereo off.

"I can hear this all the way down the hall in our bedroom!" I screamed. "Don't you realize it's keeping the girls awake and they need to get their rest and so do I!" Using God's name in vain, I then screamed, "Keep this G—— thing off!"

My brother Joe whistled at me as I stood there. I realized what I was wearing, but at that point, I didn't care. I was mad. Walt then got up and started screaming at me that he could listen to the music as loud as he wanted and that I better get back in the bedroom. "You don't tell me what to do!" I screamed again. "And if you turn it up again, I'll throw it through the wall!"

At that point, Joe and Tim got up and said they were going to leave.

"NO!" shouted Walt. "I'm leaving!"

"Fine go! See if I care!" I shouted, and I turned and ran into the bedroom. Joe and Tim got into their car and drove off. Walt climbed into his Nova and peeled out. He was furious at me and not just because of the music. None of them were in any condi-tion to drive, but I didn't care. I was furious myself. I went back and tried to calm down so I could get the girls to go back to sleep after that. They did, and then I called Cathy.

"I'm so mad! Why couldn't he just turn the music down? See what I mean, Cathy? It's impossible to live with his drinking. He just gets so stupid!"

"Maybe he drinks to get away from all your fighting," stated Cathy.

"Maybe, but that's what causes the fighting! I just can't stand him drunk anymore!" I cried.

"Maybe he's not happy in his work. You said it's gotten worse since he started at Cal-Wood Doors," she suggested.

"Yeah, it has. He started drinking at bars, and now it's nonstop. I was so mad tonight I even used God's name in vain, Cathy," I whispered shamefully.

"You need to pray, Patty, and ask God to forgive you for that and for how you treated Walt," she firmly replied.

"But he caused it!" I said.

"It doesn't matter what he did," she continued. "You should know better and be an example. Just take some time and pray, and you'll see how God can help." So I said good-bye to her and knelt beside my bed and began to pray.

"Lord," I started, "please forgive me. I should never have used your name in vain, and please forgive me for getting so mad at Walt. But I just can't stand it anymore. Please save him. Why can't things be different? I thought they would be after I was saved, but they only get worse." I then got up and walked into the girls' room to check on them.

They were sleeping soundly. They were so precious and inno-cent. They didn't deserve any of this. They were so young. June was three, and Mandy was one. They looked like angels lying in their beds.

I walked into the kitchen to get a drink of water. I had been crying now for what seemed like hours. I looked out the window at the carport and didn't see Walt's car. He hadn't gotten back yet, and I felt very worried.

I slowly walked back into our bedroom with a heavy heart. I called Cathy again and told her Walt still wasn't home. "What if he gets into an accident?" I questioned worriedly. Again, she directed me to pray. "Thanks, Cathy. I will. Good night," I said.

"Good night, and I'll be praying too," she replied.

"Lord," I prayed as I lay down on our bed, "please protect Walt. It's his fault I got so mad, but please protect him. He's just so drunk." How long I prayed, I'm not sure; but suddenly, I was aware of a presence.

CHAPTER 2

This kind of awareness had happened to me before. Some of those, I realized as good, such as the time I went to a "Jesus Freak" meeting with Cathy. The meetings were dubbed "Jesus Freak" meetings because they were not your typical Bible studies.

Cathy was about seventeen at the time, and I was around thirteen. She had attended these meetings a couple of times and asked me if I'd like to go with her. My friend Vicky Vessel was with me at the time, and so I asked if she could go too.

"Sure," said Cathy.

"I'll have to go ask my parents," Vicky replied.

"I should ask Dad too," I said, and so we did.

After Vicky called and let us know it was all right with her parents, Cathy and I drove over in Cathy's yellow Chevy LUV truck and picked her up from her house. Cathy waited in the truck as I went to the door and got Vicky. We told her parents when we thought when we'd be back, and off we went.

We drove up in front of an old Victorian house. There were many of these in La Verne as well as older adobe-style houses and, of course, the newer-styled houses. This one had a large front porch, and as we entered, I vaguely remember that we entered into what once was the living room. Now it was the central meeting room.

Cathy brought us to meet some of her acquaintances. Then she brought us to meet what seemed to be the leader. After we said hi, he instructed two guys to take Vicky and me into the next room. (I'll call them Steve and Mike, but we were never given their names.) Cathy started to follow us, but the leader stopped her and told her to wait out here, saying it would only be a short while. She did, but with a bit of hesitancy.

Mike opened the door that led into the next room, which was directly off the main room. There was what seemed like a table with short legs, and we were told to sit down on the floor around it. I went around the corner and sat on the floor, and Vicky sat on the floor just the other side of that corner. *I wonder what that was about*, I thought to myself when they wouldn't let Cathy come with us.

As Mike came around the table to my side, Steve reached out and turned off the light.

"Hey! Wait a minute!" I exclaimed quietly.

"Oh, don't worry. Nothing is going to happen. Just relax," Steve said as he reached now for the door and started to close it. Vicky and I looked at each other questionably.

As the door started to close, a hand reached in and stopped it. I couldn't hear what was being said, but I did notice how the guy who had stopped the door looked, at least what I could see.

He was wearing a light-blue button-down shirt with light tan pants. There seemed to be a bright light all around him. *Strange*, I thought. The light didn't seem that bright when we were in the main meeting room before.

Well, Steve tried once again to close the door. This time, I heard what was said.

"No! Now!" the stranger firmly said.

So Steve turned to us and asked, "Is one of you named Vicky Vessel?"

"Yes. That's my name," answered Vicky.

"Your father called and says you are to go home, now," he stated as he relayed the message from the one outside the door.

"My father?" questioned Vicky.

"That's what he said. Ya got to go now," answered Steve.

That was strange indeed! For one thing, Vicky lived with her mother and stepfather. Second, she never called him Father. It was usually by his first name, Roger, or occasionally she'd refer to him as her stepdad, so we were led out of the room.

I went to Cathy and told her we had to leave.

"Wait!" she said. "They're just getting started."

"Well, Vicky's dad called and said we are to come home, now," I said.

"Really?" questioned Cathy.

"Yes," I replied, and so she said her good-byes, and we climbed back into her truck and drove off.

"Why did your father call for us to come home?" Cathy questioned Vicky as we drove down Bonita Ave.

"I don't know," was her reply.

"Wait a minute, Vicky. How did he get the phone number?" Cathy questioned further.

"I thought you gave it to him," Vicky said.

"I didn't. Did you, Patty?" Cathy asked me.

"No, how could I? You never gave it to me," I replied.

"Well, that's funny. I don't have it," Cathy quietly responded.

"Patty, go up and find out how he got the phone number," she told me as we pulled up in Vicky's driveway. So I did.

We climbed out of the truck and entered Vicky's house.

"Well, we're home," shouted Vicky. Her parents came into the living room from the kitchen.

"Hi. Hey, Roger," I started. "We were wondering how you got the phone number to call and have us come home."

"What number?" he questioned me. "I never called for you to come home. As a matter of fact, I was wondering why you were home so soon."

"You mean you never called?" I questioned.

"Like I said, I never had the phone number," he said.

"Well, someone called and told us that it was you and that you wanted us home," I said.

"It must have been your father, Patty," Roger stated.

"Yeah, I guess so," I was saying.

Then Vicky interrupted and said, "No, they asked for me and said it was my father."

"That's right," I said.

"All I can say is, it wasn't me," replied Roger.

So I went back and relayed the conversation to Cathy.

As we drove home, I asked Cathy how Roger had gotten the phone number. She didn't know since she didn't know it herself. Then there was the fact that the stranger asked for Vicky and said it was her father who called. From that moment on, we drove in silence the rest of the way home, pondering the strange occurrence.

On another occasion, I was walking home from what was our end-of-the-school-year picnic. It was our last year at Ramona Junior High, and we celebrated at San Dimas Park. We had finished with a water balloon fight, and the park maintenance said we had better pick up every last scrap of balloon. So after we were done with that, some of us wanted to continue the fun at Kuhn's Park. That was quite a way's away, so those who had bikes let others ride as passengers on the fenders or, as in my case, on the handlebars.

We had all worn our swimsuits under our clothes, so since my T-shirt was soaked, I took it off on the trip to Kuhn's Park. I rode on my friend's handlebars for quite a while. We were lagging behind, so I hopped off and told him to ride on ahead and I'd hitchhike the rest of the way.

"No!" he said. "You can ride with me."

"No, it's okay. I can hitchhike. I'll be fine," I arrogantly stated. "See Jimmy and Mike up there?" I started as I pointed to two other friends who were walking ahead of us. "Tell them to wait for me if they get a ride and I'll pick them up if I get a ride, okay?"

"Okay, if you're sure," he said and rode off.

I put my thumb up in the air and proceeded to try to hitch a ride. This was something my parents never would have approved of, and I was watching the cars, hoping that no one my parents knew would drive by. I walked for a few miles and wasn't more than a mile from the park when I had to turn off the main high-way onto the road that led to Kuhn's Park.

As I walked through the bare dirt corner of road, a beat-up white car pulled into the dirt. "Need a ride?" questioned the guy in the backseat of the car. He had long stringy dirty blonde hair, I noticed as he leaned out the window to talk to me. The car was loaded with guys with hardly room for one more. As I looked in, I could tell that they had all been smoking pot and were com-pletely wasted.

"Can you pick up my friends up there?" I questioned as I pointed to Jimmy and Mike, who were a distance ahead of me.

"No can do!" exclaimed the guy in the backseat. "We only have room for you," he said with a grin on his face.

"Well, I guess I'll pass," I said, and I explained the previous arrangements I made with my friends.

After taking a drag off the joint he was pinching, he smiled at me and said, "You sure?"

"I'm sure," I said.

"Okay then, if you're sure. Here take this," he said as he handed me what was left of the joint, just a stub.

"Thanks. Bye," I said as they drove off. "What am I suppose to do with this?" I said out loud to no one in particular as I started to walk again. I could have dropped it, but as usual, I wanted to be cool.

As I pondered the thought, a car pulled up to the curb next to me. It seemed to me as if it had made an impossible turn to get on that road since it had turned left in a place where no left turn was possible! I was a bit taken aback when they stopped but stood at ease at once.

I noticed, this time, the car was much like the one my parents drove. It was a Ford Country Lane station wagon, very neat and clean and so were the two men in the front seat. As a matter of fact, they were wearing suits! This was very strange indeed as it was summertime in Southern California and hot! They asked me if I needed a ride.

"Yes, but can you stop and give my friends just up the road there a ride?" I questioned, and then I explained our arrangement we had made.

"Yes, we can. Just get in and lock the door," the passenger said.

"Thanks!" I exclaimed and proceeded to scoot over behind the driver so the others would have room to sit. I then locked the door as I was instructed.

As I did, a thought came to my mind. They didn't have to stop! They could just keep on driving and kidnap me! What fear came into my heart at that moment! I looked up and noticed the passenger looking at me. His eyes seemed angry and full of fire.

That was strange, and I was frightened, but as I looked over at the driver, a peace came over me. I couldn't make out his face, but I knew it was going to be all right even though I was still thinking they didn't have to stop. I was thinking of just how stupid I was when he then stopped and picked up Jimmy and Mike. What relief came into my heart at that moment.

They took us straight to the park from there. As I climbed out my door, Mike and Jimmy climbed out the other side. They walked around the front of the car and came over to me. I handed Jimmy the stub of the joint and turned to say "thank you," and the car was gone.

"Jimmy!" I exclaimed. "Where are they?" He turned and was as baffled as me.

"I don't know!" he said. We both ran down the street to see if they could have made it up to the corner and turned even though it had literally only been five seconds.

"They are nowhere!" I exclaimed again. "How can that be?" I questioned as I once again thought of the look of anger from the passenger and the feeling of peace from the driver.

I truly believe that in both of these occasions, God had intervened for me and prevented a very bad situation from happening. I feel as if the presence of the unexpected man at the "Jesus Freak" meeting and these two gentlemen who picked me up were angels unknown to me, sent to protect me and the others with me. On another occasion though, the presence was not good and such fear filled my heart.

CHAPTER 3

It was summer vacation for all the kids in the neighborhood. I was twelve years old at the time. We had been having a great time in the warm California summer months. There were games in our front yard most days since we had the largest yard on the block. Games such as red rover and Crockett, and we played baseball in the dead-end street and went to the neighborhood pool.

It was sometime in midsummer vacation that we all decided to have a séance. Later that day, Colleen, my girl friend from next door, and I had decided to ask the Ouija board game who would come and speak through one of us at the séance. I had taken it to her house since there were too many kids at mine.

Now we played with this game just as many other people do. It was just a game to us, and we honestly did not believe in any "power" behind it. Soon, we found out that there was.

As we asked it questions, such as where to have the séance and when, it would spell out the answer for us. We had lightly placed our fingers on the triangle, as the instructions told us to and as we had done many times before. The "game" answered us that we were to gather at Colleen's living room at 6 p.m. that day. Then we asked who would be speaking during the gathering. This is when it became too real.

As we asked the question, I was thinking it would spell out Abraham Lincoln. That was who we pretended "appeared" all the other times we had a séance. As my eyes went to the letter *A*, expecting the triangle to move there, it moved in a circle as usual and then moved a bit forcibly under my fingers to the letter *M* and stopped. I looked up at Colleen, and she looked up at me.

"I guess it's going to be Moses," I said with a bit of a chuckle.

"Yeah, guess so," Colleen replied with a smile. The triangle moved in a circle again, and then quickly, it moved to the letter *E*.

"Me?" I questioned.

"Why did you move it to that?" I asked Colleen.

"I didn't move it there. I thought you did," she replied.

"Well, if you didn't move it there and I didn't, who did?" I nervously asked her.

"I guess whoever *Me* is," she said and then laughed a short nervous laugh.

"Yeah! Sure! Me, whoever that is," I repeated and laughed nervously as well.

"What should we ask next?" Colleen asked me.

"I guess we should see who Me will be speaking through," I answered.

So we proceeded to ask the game, "Who will you be speaking through?" What happened next is the honest terrifying truth.

The triangle moved in a circle as before. Then one by one, it chose the letters *P, A,* and *T* and hesitated a brief moment. I figured it was Pat, who was one of our friends who was meeting with us that night. But then, it started moving in a circle and glided over *T* once again.

"NO!" I screamed. "Not me!" I jumped up in fear. As the board and triangle fell to the floor, I screamed at Colleen, "Why did you move it to my name?"

"I didn't, Patty!" she shouted back.

"Yes, you did because I had my fingers barely over the top. I wasn't even touching it!" I continued to shout.

"Me too! I wasn't touching it either!" Colleen said.

I just kept screaming that he couldn't come through me. I grabbed Colleen, pushed her down, and hollered, "You moved it! You had to have moved it! It doesn't do that on its own!"

"But I didn't move it! Honest! Are you sure you didn't?" she asked me.

"I'm sure!" I said in a bit quieter voice. I began to cry uncontrollably.

"Well, if it wasn't you and it surely wasn't me, then who moved it?" I cried out.

"I guess whoever Me is," she stated in a hushed tone.

"But who is that?" I questioned. Then a deep dark fear filled me, and I screamed. I said I wasn't coming to the gathering and no one was speaking through me.

"We won't do it, Patty. We will just cancel it," Colleen said.

"Sure we will," said Kathy, Colleen's older sister who came in when I screamed. "Just calm down," she said as she put an arm around my shoulder, "and go home for now. It's not real, Patty."

"It is real!" I shouted at her. "Colleen didn't move it, and neither did I." I grabbed the board, barely able to touch it without fear, and ran home.

When I reached home, which was just next door, I threw the game down and ran to my room. The fear overwhelmed me again, and I screamed for my sister. "Barbara! Help me! He can't come through me! He can't!" I said as I cried out.

"Who? What are to talking about 'he can't come through you'?" Barbara questioned me as she ran into the room. I then told her what had happened as I cried hysterically. "Please, Barbara! Don't let it happen!" I pleaded with her.

Barbara was the second oldest in our family, and we were very close at the time. We shared the master bedroom and had shared a bedroom for most of our lives. Barbara was my hero, you could say, as she was always sticking up for me and protecting me. Whenever I needed her, she was there for me.

Barbara grabbed me at that time and tried to calm me down. She told me it was just a game and not to worry. I told her it was for real, that neither Colleen nor I had moved it and if I had, why would I move it to my name? She suggested that Colleen could have and just not told me.

"No way!" I exclaimed. "I asked her, and she swears she did not move it either."

"But who is Me?" asked Barbara.

"I don't know," I moaned. "But I am sure it's not good! He can't come through me, Barbara! He can't!"

"Well, who's he?" she asked again.

"I don't know!" I once again moaned, but then I stopped to think about the answer and horror filled my heart. "What if it's the devil?" I said in a deep throated voice. When that thought hit me, I looked with fear at Barbara.

"No," said Barbara.

"It must be! Who else can it mean!?" I stated, and then I started to scream and cry again.

"Look, Patty. Just lay down and rest. You're getting hysterical. You'll feel better if you sleep a bit," Barbara said as she laid my head down.

"But you won't leave me, will you?" I asked her.

"I'll stay right here. Don't worry and go to sleep," she answered.

I lay there and closed my eyes, then as I felt sleep coming on, I jumped up. "Barbara!" I cried.

"I'm right here," she reassured me.

"Please don't let him get me! Please!" I pleaded with her.

"No one is going to get you. I won't leave you," she reassured me.

I felt safe with her there and was able to finally doze off in a fitful sleep but not before I heard her say that she was going to call Mom.

We never called Mom at work, but Barbara felt that this was too much, and she needed to find out what Mom wanted her to do. After a while, I awoke and found Mom and Barbara talking.

When Mom had gotten home, she asked Barbara exactly what had happened. I heard her reply, "I don't know, Mom. She just came home freaking out and saying that he couldn't come through her."

"Who's he, and what does she mean 'come through her'?" asked Mom. So Barbara tried the best she could to fill Mom in with what she knew.

As I awoke, I jumped out of bed and started to cry. "I can't fall asleep again! What if he came to me in my sleep?"

"Stop being ridiculous, Patty! No one's going to get you when you sleep," Mom said, trying to calm me down.

"But he will! I know he will!" I said, and then I fell apart and started to cry hysterically once again.

Mom came over and wrapped her arms around me. "My god!" she exclaimed. "She's shaking like a leaf! I'm calling your father." She then had me come into the living room and sit on the couch. I wouldn't let Barbara leave me as I was still terrified.

Soon, my dad came home and asked what was going on. Mom filled him in on what had transpired. She had called and talked to Colleen, and Colleen had verified all I had said had happened.

My dad called me over to where Mom and he had been talking. "Explain to me exactly what happened, Patty," he said. So I told him how it had transpired at Colleen's house.

"Why are you afraid?" he asked. "Because it spelled out my name, and he's going to come through me!" I said.

"But you decided not to have a séance right? So why are you still afraid?" he asked me.

"Because I think he'll come to me in my sleep, Dad. I just can't shake that feeling!" I moaned.

So Dad took the game out of the cupboard and started to walk down the hall.

"What are you going to do?" asked Mom.

"I'm going to throw it out in the trash," Dad said.

Later, I walked out to see it in the trash for myself. I needed to be reassured it was out of our house, and my life, but it wasn't there. I asked Mom where Dad had put it.

"In the trash, Patty. Now let it go!" she said a bit exasperated. This whole ordeal was a bit exasperating.

"But it's not in the trash. Honest, Mom. I just went and looked," I stated.

"Why would you do that?" she asked as she walked outside to where the trash was kept.

"I just wanted to be sure it was gone. That's all," I said, a bit subdued.

As we reached the trash cans, Mom could see that the game was in fact not there. She then came inside and asked Dad why he hadn't thrown it away. She could tell I was still very afraid.

"Mary Ann, I did throw it away," Dad replied.

"Where?" Mom asked him.

"In the trash," he said, a bit annoyed. I think they both thought that this was just something I was overreacting about.

Mom asked if it was our trash he had thrown it in. "Of course, Mary Ann."

"It's not there, Russ," Mom said with bit of a look of bewilderment in her eyes.

"I threw it in our trash!" said Dad as he proceeded to go check.

As Dad went to check the trash, Mom and Barbara went to the hallway cupboard where we kept our games. There it was! Near the top of the stack!

"Russ!" shouted Mom.

"What!" exclaimed Dad.

"It's right here!" she told him.

"It can't be! I know I threw it away," he was saying as he entered the hallway. He looked up and said in a hushed voice, "Well, I'll be! I know for a fact I threw it in the trash. How did it get back in there? Did one of the kids put it back?" he asked a bit upset.

"No," replied Mom. "I've already asked while you were outside checking the trash can, and besides, which one could have put it way up there? You'd need a step stool yourself," Mom said, amazed.

My dad was six foot three, and most definitely, he would have needed a step stool to accomplish the task. Mom was right. No one could have put it back there and, not to mention, without someone noticing. "How could it get up there then?" Dad asked.

"I don't know, Russ," answered Mom. "Do you think we should call Father John?"

Father John was our parish priest from the Catholic church we attended. After talking on the phone with Father John, Dad said that Father John suggested cutting it up, that it must have an evil power. So Dad took a kitchen chair, pushed it up to the hallway cupboard, and pulled the game out once again.

He carried it to the backyard, removed it from the box, and leaned it against a log for leverage. He then briskly walked to the garage, picked up his ax, and proceeded to the backyard to chop it up. He lifted the ax high above his head and came down hard on it. Nothing! Not even a scratch.

"Mary Ann!" exclaimed Dad. "Did you see that?" We all had been watching and couldn't believe our eyes.

"Try hitting it harder, Russ!" exclaimed Mom. So Dad lifted the heavy ax high above his head again and gave it all he had. Nothing! Again, not even a scratch.

Dad just looked up at my mom and then at me. "Mary Ann, get her out of here," he demanded quietly.

"What are you going to do?" she asked.

"I'm going to burn it in the fireplace, but I don't want her anywhere near when I do," he informed her.

"Why?" questioned Mom, and I was wondering too.

"I don't know what will happen, and I just think it's best if she's not around. Just get her and all the kids out of here."

So Mom took me and the rest of the kids out to the store, and when we came back, it was done. We never saw the Ouija board again. My father had burned it with the box and triangle as well. I felt safer but still begged Barbara to hold on to me as I fell asleep that night. I was able to finally fall asleep and had no further problems that night.

If anyone ever brings up this "harmless" game, I tell them it's not harmless and they are better off to leave it alone. This was the first time I felt evil and came to realize the reality of its power in our midst. That is exactly what I felt as I was praying that night Walt drove off because of me getting mad about the music and his drinking.

CHAPTER 4

That night, after I hung up the phone from talking with Cathy, I started to pray. I asked God to keep Walt safe and to forgive me for my attitude toward Walt.

"Lord, I know I was wrong. I didn't think about walking out in my nightie, but I was so mad! Why couldn't he just turn down the music?" I tried to reason. It showed just how infantile I was in my walk with God. I didn't know just how far I still was from God, and I was soon to find out.

I was still praying when I sensed the presence. "It's no use praying," a voice hissed. I started to pray again. "It's no use," the voice hissed again. I lifted my head from off the pillow and looked across the room.

There, standing next to the opened door of our master bathroom was a figure! A female figure. I could only see the silhouette as the light was off in our bedroom, but our next-door neighbors' porch light was on and shining through the frosted glass window above our vanity.

I asked who it was. It just smiled a Cheshire Cat smile at me. Fear filled my heart.

"It's no use praying, Patty," said the figure. "God won't hear you."

"Yes, he will," I retorted.

"Walt's been in an accident and won't be coming home," it said.

"I'll call Cathy, and she will help me pray," I said as I picked up the phone. I dialed her number, and then the phone went dead.

I must have not waited for the dial tone, I thought, so I hung up the receiver and waited a few seconds. I picked up the phone again, waited for the dial tone, and dialed her number. Nothing. Once again, I laid the phone on the receiver, picked it up, dialed slowly, and nothing!

I then looked back at the figure, and it started to laugh a hideous laugh. I could see the eyes, and they were red and slanted like Cheshire Cat. "It's no use! No one is here to help you!" it said. I sat up, filled with such a fear. Suddenly, the figure flew straight at me in a swishing movement.

"God!" I cried out, "No!" as it came right at me. Just as I cried out to God, the figure disappeared! It was gone, and I was sitting wide awake in my bed. I turned and jumped out of my bed. I ran to grab the phone, and I dialed Cathy once again. This time, it rang, and she answered.

"Cathy!" I screamed and started to cry.

"What, Patty?" she asked.

"I am so glad you answered!" I cried. "I've tried and tried to call you, but it wouldn't let me."

"It?" she questioned. "What do you mean?" I then told her what had just transpired in my bedroom. "Honest, Cathy. It really happened! I'm still afraid! What am I supposed to do? What do you think happened? Do you think something happened to Walt?" I cried out.

"Calm down, Patty. God is greater than anything. He'll be with Walt. Let's pray right now," she said comfortingly. So we prayed for God's protection on Walt and that God's presence would be with me in a real way.

"Now," continued Cathy, "go check on the girls."

"Okay," I replied. "But stay on the line. I'll try to keep the phone with me if the phone cord will reach their room." This was way before cordless phones or cell phones.

I quickly walked against the wall as far away from our bathroom as possible. As I entered the hallway, the fearful feeling was gone! "Strange," I said under my breath.

"What?" questioned Cathy.

"The bad feeling was gone the minute I stepped out of my bedroom."

"That's good. How are the girls?" she asked.

"I'll have to put the phone down on the washer. It won't reach all the way," I said, and I laid it on the washer, which was in the hall between our bedroom and the girls' bedroom.

I walked in and felt complete peace as I did. I walked over to each of their beds and bent down to see that they were sound asleep. They were so innocent! They were so precious to me! I silently thanked God for protecting them from whatever had been in my room. I lightly placed a kiss on each of their cheeks and whispered "I love you." I walked out and picked up the phone once again.

"They're fine. Sound asleep," I said a bit more settled.

"Good," replied Cathy. "Now go back in your room and continue to pray for Walt."

"But what if it comes back?" I asked fearfully.

"It won't. God was there when you called out. Evil cannot be there if God is," she said reassuringly.

So I hesitantly walked into our bedroom. "It feels bad again, Cathy!" I said as I stepped back into the hallway.

"Just go in. We can pray as you do," she said.

"Okay, but you pray," I said. She started to pray, and I walked slowly back into the bedroom.

"Will you please stay on the line while I check around my room?" I asked a bit shakily.

"All right. I will. Just pray with me as you do," she said, and as I walked through my room checking every corner, closet, and the bathroom, we prayed. We pleaded for the blood of Christ and asked God for peace.

I finally lay back in my bed and asked Cathy to stay on the line with me.

"Just lay down and we'll continue to pray," she answered. We continued to pray for a while, and then I finally said, "It's okay now, Cathy. Thank you, and I'm sorry I woke you up and kept you up so late."

"That's all right," she reassured me. "Just pray for Walt and focus on him as you pray, and you'll go to sleep."

I said good night and hung up the phone.

"Lord, please don't let anything happen to Walt. Thank you for your help tonight. I don't know where Walt is, but I'm going to trust you. Thank you again," I prayed as I fell asleep.

The next morning, Walt came home. I ran out to him and threw my arms around him. "I'm so glad you came home! I'm so sorry for being so stupid! But you made me so mad!" I said.

"I was mad at you too!" Walt said.

"You shouldn't have come out in your nightie. That made me so mad."

"I know. It was wrong of me. I just wasn't thinking. Where were you all night? Where did you go?" I asked.

"My car ran off the road. I was driving about sixty to seventy miles per hour. I can't believe I didn't total the car. It took me all night to get it out," he said. I asked him about when it had happened. When he told me the time, it was exactly when Cathy and I were praying for his protection. God is so faithful!

Well, after that night, our life went on just as always. Walt continued to drink, yet he worked hard at his job. He was home each night, yet we seemed to drift further apart.

I was trying to be the best mother and wife I could be. I continued to become a better housekeeper and took better care of myself. I was quite lonely though, and having a drunken husband most of the time only added to my distress. No matter what I did, I wasn't receiving any love from Walt. I would pray that things would change for us. Something had to or our marriage wasn't going to make it.

CHAPTER 5

It was now December 1978. We had celebrated Mandy's first birthday with a wonderful party. Walt's mother, father, and younger brother, Bill, were there to help celebrate. There was cake, ice cream, a barbeque, family, and friends. It was a good time. Mom and Pop Meyer and Bill left a few days afterward, but before they did, we had made plans to come and visit them for the New Year celebration and were looking forward to doing so.

During that same December, Donna Reischman, who was a girlfriend from high school and married to Walt's best friend, Rick, called me. Walt and Rick had been friends since the beginning of high school. Donna and I were friends, but I was surprised to be hearing from her.

"Hi, Patty. This is Donna," she started out.

"Well, hi, Donna!" I exclaimed. "How are you?"

"Good! As a matter of fact, I got saved and wanted to tell you," she replied. "I need to tell you I'm sorry for stealing your paper back in school and ask you to forgive me," she went on.

"Oh, that's fine. It was a long time ago! Don't worry about it. Hey, and guess what?" I excitedly said. "I'm saved too!"

"Really?" questioned Donna.

"Yeah!" I said. "I went with my sister Cathy to a service and got saved!"

"That's great!" she replied.

"Oh! And guess what?" I asked her.

"What?" she replied.

"We are coming out to visit Walt's parents for New Year's. Can you and Rick come over?"

"I guess so," she said. "I'll ask Rick and let you know."

"Great! It'll be so good to see you guys again!" I replied, and then we said our good-byes and hung up the phone.

It was so like me to not even consider if Walter's parents wanted people over or not. I never took time to consider anyone else. In my defense though, Mom and Pop always seemed to open their home to Walter's or Bill's friends, so in retrospect, I just assumed it was all right.

The day after Christmas, we were making the trip down to visit with Mom and Pop and reconnect with our friends. After a couple of days, my best friend from high school, Vicki Peters, called me. She said her mom had seen me and Walt and had let her know we were in town. Vicki was now Vicki Babb as she had gotten married after Walt and I had moved. Her husband's name was Joe, and they had a sweet little one-year-old girl named Tamra.

I just had to ask if it was all right to invite others to Mom and Pop's house, besides Rick and Donna, for the New Year's. "Vicki called and I would like to see her again, Walt. Besides, we can meet her husband as well," I told him. I wanted to have a New Year's party like always. One with drinking and plenty of food and friends! Again, I was so inconsiderate of Mom and Pop, yet they said it was all right and really was looking forward to seeing all our friends too. They were loving people who were loved by everyone.

Well, Vicki asked if Joe's cousin Daniel could come with them. I asked and was given the okay by Mom and Pop. That evening started out like all the other parties.

Everyone was so excited to see one another. I was so happy to be with my two friends and their husbands. Walt and I had been married five years already, so it was good to see my friends married. Donna was expecting their second child, Vicki had one little girl, and I had two little girls. Vicki and Donna had found babysitters, but June Ann and Mandy Lyn were, of course, with us as we were staying at Walt's parents' house.

I'll never forget that evening. We all proceeded to eat, drink, and be "merry"—all, that is, but Donna. I was dressed in what I considered a nice outfit—black dress slacks and a sheer printed blouse. Walt wasn't too happy with my choice, but I never considered what he thought of anymore. I had lost respect for him, and he for me. Vicki was wearing a nice pants outfit, and Donna had corduroy maternity pants suit on. It was strange seeing her dressed so modestly as this wasn't the Donna I was used to.

As we continued into the night, I noticed Donna wasn't drinking. *Guess it's because she's expecting*, I thought. Yet there seemed something more. She seemed happy with Rick, which was unusual for her, and she seemed at peace.

We had briefly talked about getting saved. I noticed Vicki smile questionably, and I didn't want to ruin the party mood, so I quickly changed the subject. *After all*, I thought, *I'm saved, but I can have fun too*. But with Donna, it was different. Why, I didn't know, but she really shined for Jesus.

That evening, as the New Year's party wore on, I noticed Donna sitting off from the rest of us. As I looked over at her, I sensed a presence surrounding her. She almost glowed! I didn't know what to make of it, but I knew she was different. She had changed. *She really seems different than me*, I thought. Soon, I would get a chance to find out just what Donna had.

CHAPTER 6

It was during that party that Walt asked Joe what he did for a living.

"I work in construction," Joe replied.

"Me too," stated Walt. "I am working in a factory though and I hate it."

"I build houses in the High Desert with my uncle's company. I love what I do," Joe replied.

"Man, I'd love to build houses," Walt said with a gleam in his eye. I knew he was unhappy with his work, so I picked up on the conversation and listened intently.

"Well, why don't you work building houses then?" Joe asked.

"I don't know," was Walt's reply. "Hey, do you think I could work with you? Do you guys have any openings?"

"I don't know. I'll ask Daniel since his dad's the owner." So Joe asked Daniel, who said he'd have to ask his dad.

The party ended, and everyone headed home. No one got too drunk as we were too busy visiting and really having a great time. I was grateful to see Walt not drunk and to have reunited with my friends.

Within a couple of days, Joe called Walt and told him that his uncle wanted to meet him.

"Just come up and talk to him," he told Walt.

"All right, but when?" asked Walt.

"Tomorrow, he wants to meet you. I put in a good word for you, and I think he'll hire you," replied Joe.

"Great!" Walt exclaimed. "See you tomorrow." He got directions to the meeting place in the High Desert where the business was located.

I was very excited for this to happen. Walt had hated working in the factorylike setting of the door company, and his increased drinking proved it. I had hoped that this would be the change he needed, and I told him so as we discussed it before his meeting with Warren, who was Joe's uncle and the owner of the company.

"Are you sure this is what you want?" I asked him.

"Yeah! I really would like to build houses, but Joe says the pay is four dollars an hour. That's a dollar less an hour than I'm making now, and there are no benefits," he replied.

"I don't care. We can manage if it'll make you happy. You can't continue at what you're doing. I can't stand how miserable you are, and you are making me miserable!" I said as I chuckled a bit. So he went the next day and got the job! We were both so excited!

We asked his parents if we could move in with them since we wouldn't have enough time or money to get our own place. "It should only be for a couple of months," Walt said. "By then we should be able to save enough to get our own apartment." As I said before, Mom and Pop would do anything to help their kids, and so we moved into their house by the end of January 1979.

There was Walter, myself, and two children living with Mom, Pop, Bill, and Walt's niece Christina in a two-bedroom, one-bathroom house. Not to mention, all our furniture and belongings on the back-covered porch and garage. The girls slept on the Hide A Bed in the dinning room, while Walter and I slept on a single bed in Bill's bedroom. I think back now and realize just how difficult this must have been for everyone, but then I could only think of how difficult it was for me.

I wasn't doing anything spiritually at the time. As a matter of fact, I had slipped back into my sinful ways, or had I ever left them? I allowed myself to feel abandoned by Walt, who was busy driving sixty miles every day to and from work. His mom was constantly telling me how to be a better wife, and if I didn't meet her standards, she just did it herself.

For instance, once, she made Walt lunch when he told me he didn't want one. I had asked him what he wanted, and he told me, "It's too hot outside, and the sandwich just gets nasty after a while." I told his mom this, but she didn't believe me.

Another time, I wanted to make dinner, but Mom wouldn't have it. I now realize it was because she was used to doing the cooking and cleaning, but she just wouldn't let me be the housewife. The old saying is so true! "You can't have two women running the same house." Well, it was her house, but understanding this didn't help me at all.

Since I felt pushed aside and never had time alone with Walt, my desires almost got the best of me. Once, I felt like cheating on Walt, but as soon as I realized what was happening, I stopped the thought and removed myself from the situation.

That night, when Walt came home, I begged him to find a place for us.

"How?" he asked. "We haven't saved up enough." As a matter of fact, we hadn't saved anything. We spent the money almost as fast as it came in.

"I don't care how. We just have to move now!" I replied anxiously. "You don't understand!" I continued. "I can't do this anymore. I never get time alone with you, and I can't be the wife and mother I want to be."

"I guess I'll ask Dad if he can help us get into a place," Walt said. Later that week, he did just that.

As the week wore on, I was beside myself with guilt. "How could you even think of doing such a thing as cheating on Walt?" came the question. "You're a terrible wife and mother. You can't do anything right!" continued the accusing voice in my head.

"That's right!" I said to myself. "I am horrible! I can't do anything right. I'll just go out and get stone drunk and kill myself," I said, and I meant it. I was defeated. Why go on? Walt and the girls would be better off without me. And so was my plan, but God had other plans for me.

You see, Donna had truly changed, and she wanted to help me find the peace she had. She had been coming over and visiting with me. I was trying to act the Christian part, but God saw me and knew exactly where I was and would soon help me find a real relationship with him. This is what I lacked, a relationship with God, but I didn't realize it.

Once while Donna and I were discussing the Bible, she told me that to be a Catholic was sinful.

"No way! I'm Catholic, and I'm a Christian!" I retorted.

"Yes, but did you know it says not to bow down to any statues in worship, and that's what Catholics do," she answered me.

"No, they don't. We only do it to help us pray. Besides, it's statues of Mary, Joseph, and Jesus on the cross," I responded.

"Let's look at it," she said as she opened her Bible. "Here in Exodus chapter 20, starting in verse 4. You read it."

"You read it," I returned.

"No, it's important you see for yourself," she wisely stated.

So I began to read out loud, "Thou shalt not make unto thee any graven image, or any likeness of any thing that is in heaven above, or that is in the earth beneath, or that is in the water under the earth, thou shalt not bow down thyself to them nor serve them: for I the Lord thy God am a jealous God."

As I read the verses, a light started to come on in my heart. "Well, we don't worship the statues, and it is Jesus and his mother Mary after all," I said, a bit more subdued.

"Yes, but it says not to bow down to any image of anything in heaven or earth. This includes any statues of Mary, or of Jesus on the cross even," she stated.

I had to admit that it did say that even though at first I had said it didn't, but I really had no idea what the Bible said. "Well, why don't you pray and ask God to help you understand the Bible," Donna asked me.

I then asked, "Can we really know what it says?"

"Sure! God helps me to understand it every day," she said. "And he wants to help you too." I had to admit again that I was blind when it came to things of God. I really wanted what Donna had but couldn't understand just how anyone could know the things of God.

"How do you know God is talking with you?" I asked.

"He lets me know. Why don't you come to our revival meeting tonight?" she came out and asked.

"Church on Thursday? What's revival?" I questioned.

"This is a special service where we meet for wonderful preaching. If you come, you might find out what you want to know. It's a good church full of good Christians, Patty. You'll like it I'm sure," she continued.

My heart did so want what she had, whatever that was. "Well, I am a Christian after all," I had reasoned. Then I said, "All right. I'll go, but I'll have to pick you up to go with me. I don't know the way. When does it start?"

"It starts at 7 p.m., so you can pick me up around 6:30," Donna said as she left to get in their car and head home with Rick.

"Well, I'm going to church with Donna tonight," I informed Walt as I went back into the house.

"No, you're not," he challenged me.

"Oh, yes I am! I already told her I was, and besides, it's church! And I'm taking the car. It's not like we're going out drinking," I said stubbornly. Yet in the back of my mind, I remembered the plan I had made to do just that, and worse, but I'd give God a try one more time, I reasoned within myself.

"I'll go to whatever church you want me to," I reasoned with God. "Just show me where." So it was left in God's hands, even if I didn't really understand that I was communicating with God and he with me.

Later, after making sure the girls were fed, changed, and ready for bed, I climbed into the Nova and drove off. Walt wasn't happy, but oh well. I didn't care much about what Walt wanted. I drove to Pamona, where Donna lived, and picked her up. We drove to the next town over which was Upland and up to a very small white building with the words "Bible Covenant Church" on the sign.

"Not like the churches you're used to, huh, Patty?" questioned Donna.

"No," was all I said.

"Don't let the size fool you. God meets with us, and we are blessed. Even in this small building." A bit strange, I thought, but I want to see what's up with Donna, so here I am. Then after meeting the pastor's wife, we walked into the church.

There was a center isle, wooden pews, and a small platform with a pulpit in the center of that. Each side of the room had five or six rows of seven-foot pews. There were songbooks like I had never seen before in the wooden pockets located on the back of each pew. There were Sunday school rooms, I was told, in the back along with the restrooms. And there were no statues of any kind.

As we came in, Donna guided me to the center of the pews on the right. She slid in first, then I slid in next to her. She introduced me to some ladies as they came up to me and shook my hand. The pastor came over and asked, "Who's your friend, Donna?"

"This is Patty. She moved here from Northern California. We've been friends for a while now," Donna said.

"Well, it's nice to meet you, Patty. My name is Wayne Stewry. It's our pleasure to have you worship with us."

"Thank you," I replied, and I noticed everyone called him Brother Stewry. As a matter of fact, everyone called each other brother and sister.

I noticed something else a bit different here. Everyone was very nice, but the women all wore long dresses, and the men wore plain suits. The ladies all had their hair up, and everyone carried their Bibles as easily as if they were carrying a purse.

Oh boy! I thought. *What have I gotten myself into? Well, at least Donna looks more like me. Her hair is cut, and she's wearing pants like me. She does look a bit different though. It must be that glow of pregnancy*. I continued to reason within myself. Then we began to sing.

The songs we sung were not ones that I was used to. Some were like the ones we sang in the Catholic church, but others were not. The people seemed to sing from their souls, and their faces shown as they sang.

Finally, Brother Stewry started to preach. He preached on salvation. That we must be saved to enter heaven. That salvation consists of repenting of your sins and forsaking them. He continued with his sermon, but I lost myself in thought.

I know we need to ask forgiveness, but forsaking, what is that? I continued to think of different things about my life. Things such as, if I was a Christian, how come I was such a terrible wife and mother? Why was Donna and everyone here happy in such a real way? Actually, why wasn't I as happy as them? Finally, my attention was drawn back as Brother Stewry ended his sermon with an invitation to come up front to the altar and get saved.

Everyone bowed their heads as Brother Stewry led in prayer and continued to give the invitation to get saved. I was bowing my head and feeling a battle going on in my heart when a dear little woman, Sister Browning I'd learn later, came to me, and gently touching my arm, she sweetly asked me, "Would you like to go up front to pray?"

"I'm already saved!" I shouted at her. Her face showed the shock as I turned and looked at her with a disdained look.

"Oh, I see, but do you want to pray anyways?" she gently asked me.

"No! Just leave me alone!" I said as I seethed with anger.

How dare she ask me to get saved! I thought to myself. Donna just looked over to her and gave her a sweet smile, and then she turned to me. "It's all right to go up and pray, Patty. No one will hurt you," Donna said.

"I know, but I'm already saved! I just want to go home," I told her. So Donna walked over to Sister Stewry and told her we had to go. She let her know how much I wanted out of there, and boy did I! This was all too much for me.

Soon, we were in the car and headed home. I never gave it a thought that Donna was having to leave before she wanted; I just wanted out of there, and it couldn't be soon enough!

That night, I lay in bed furious. *How dare that woman ask me to get saved!* I thought. *Why would she do that? Surely Donna told them I was saved.* Yet, I didn't see Donna get upset with me when I made such a scene. As a matter of fact, no one did. I was the only one upset.

"Why were you so upset?" came the question.

"Because they should know I'm saved!" I answered back in my thoughts.

"Just how are they suppose to know that?" the voice continued to question in my heart.

"Well, I told Donna! She should have told them!" I answered.

So the battle raged on all night. I went back and forth with the voice in my heart. It was asking pointed questions as to why I thought I was saved and how did I show it.

"I am saved because I prayed back in Calvary Chapel that night when I went with Cathy," I answered "I prayed and 'believed' just like they told me to, and I was going to the Catholic church like Walt wanted me to. Now we're here and I'm so tired of trying to figure it out!" I continued. Silence. *Well, I'm done trying. I just don't know what to do,* I thought. Then something strange happened.

"Well, you asked me to show you where to go. This is it," the voice in my heart replied.

I answered back, "Yes, I did but…" And I paused, then questioned, "There?"

"Yes, there," was the reply.

"But they are so different! You can't expect me to be like that!" I argued. There was silence. *Well, I did ask,* I thought. *I guess I'll go again only if Donna asks me to.*

Then I realized for the first time that I was talking to God. "God," I asked, "is this you?"

"Yes, child. It's me," he answered in a gentle voice.

"You mean I've been talking to you all night?" I questioned as the early morning sun began to filter in.

"Yes, you have," he answered.

"And you've been talking to me?" I asked in a quieted spirit.

"Yes, I have," he answered.

I was flabbergasted and awed all at the same time. Here it was morning and I had been talking with God all night and he with me! I didn't know what to make of it, but if God would talk to me, I would do anything he wanted. Donna called later that day, and after we talked a bit, she asked me if I would go to church with her again.

"Oh, ah, no," I said at first, then I remembered that during our talk, I had told God if Donna asked, I'd go.

"Come on, Patty. Just come one more time," she went on. I said okay but with a stipulation on it.

"If Walt lets me go, I'll go." I remembered his reaction the night before and expected wholeheartedly that he would refuse to let me go again.

"Well, go ask him," Donna said, not letting me off the hook so quickly.

"Walt," I started as I put down the phone, "Donna wants me to go to church again tonight. Is it okay with you?"

"Yeah," he replied right away.

What! I thought. "You sure you don't mind watching the girls again?" I questioned, hoping he'd be discouraged in letting me go by that.

"No, it's fine. Just go," he said. "But someone will have to pick you up. I have to change the oil in the car."

Good! I thought. *Here's my chance.* So I picked up the phone and told Donna that Walt said I could but I couldn't use the car. "That's fine. You can go with me."

"Oh, okay," I said a bit disappointingly.

"Sister Stewry is picking me up, so she'll stop by and pick you up first since I live near the church."

"No! No!" I exclaimed. "I don't even know her!"

"You met last night, and besides, that is the only way I can go. Come on, Patty. Please come with me," she so sweetly pleaded with me.

Now all my excuses were out of the way, so I had to tell her I'd go. "Fine," I said. "I'll go," I replied. I guess I'll see why God has chosen this church because I sure wouldn't have! So I hung up the phone and thought that this was all a bit strange.

CHAPTER 7

That evening, Sister Stewry picked me up promptly at 6:30. From there, we went to pick up Donna. Sister Stewry tried to make small talk, but I wasn't talkative. I was still mulling over the events of the previous night, and even those that influenced the situation I was now in.

We had picked up Donna, and I once again was disconnected from the conversation. I just wanted this night to be over with as quickly as possible. I wasn't thrilled to be there, and everyone could tell.

We entered the church after parking the car. Some came up to me and said that they were happy to see me again. Even Sister Browning greeted me with a sweet smile and gentle handshake. *Wow!* I thought. *Even after the way I treated her? Well, she shouldn't have bothered me last night, and no one better bother me tonight!*

I told Donna I wanted to sit further in the back. "You sure?" she questioned.

"Yeah. I just don't want to be bothered by anyone," I answered.

She graciously slid into the back seat, then I followed.

Good! I thought to myself. *I just can't have anyone bothering me tonight. If you have anything to show me, God, you'll have to do it so I know it's you.* Then the service began.

There was singing once again and prayer, but then as Brother Stewry started to preach, his subject was on sanctification. I listened intently as I had never heard of this before. He said we had to die to self to be sanctified. He went on to explain that it was God's Spirit we needed in our hearts to keep from sinning. Well, I knew I was still sinning even though I thought I was saved.

Die to self? I questioned within my heart, and as he continued to expand his subject, I began to have a warming of my heart. Just what was happening, I didn't know or understand, but something was transpiring in my heart for sure. Exactly what Brother Stewry said to explain sanctification, I couldn't have told you then. God was dealing with me, and I became oblivious to my surroundings.

It seemed as if I was alone with God. Suddenly, I noticed Brother Stewry was coming to an end of his sermon. "In closing," he was saying, "is there anyone who feels the need to pray?" Well, I was feeling something! Then ever so gently, God spoke to me.

"Go," he said.

"I'm scared," my heart cried.

"Go," he said once again and then added, "I will carry you all the way if you take the first step."

I thought, "All right, God. I'll go if you go with me." And I took one step out into the isle.

I don't remember even feeling my feet hit the ground after that, but suddenly, I was kneeling in front of the altar, praying. "God," I started, "I don't want one person up here, please. This has to be between you and me," was my simple request. Then it was just me and him. Later, I'd come to know that, miraculously, God kept others from coming to the altar and praying with me. God knew it had to be that way.

As I bowed my head and prayed that prayer, it seemed as if the whole world disappeared. I was surrounded by what seemed like a cloud. It was white and peaceful. I was kneeling before the altar, but there was nothing else visible to me. Then suddenly, I sensed someone standing in front of me.

I looked up and saw Jesus! I couldn't make out his facial features, but I knew it was him, and I also knew he was looking down on me with gentleness and love. He then reached out his hand to me.

I looked on that nail-pierced hand and then started to cry uncontrollably. I do not know if anyone else in the church saw me cry, but my heart ached with grief over the realization, for the first time ever, that my sin caused his suffering. I collapsed at the altar as that reality filled my heart. I moaned, "Oh God! I'm so sorry!"

"Look up child," Jesus said.

As I looked up, he reached out his nail-pierced hand once again to me. "No!" is all I could say as I leaned away. "No! I can't take your hand!"

"You must," Jesus said. Then I looked again and saw his pleading yet loving eyes.

I looked down at my clothing. I was clothed in a long white garment, much like a choir gown, and it was covered in dirt and torn. Then I said, "But I'm so filthy! I can't!"

Jesus then reached out both nail-pierced hands and gently said once again, "You must."

I was so ashamed, but I knew I must. So I placed my hand in his nail-pierced hand. He lifted me up and enfolded me in his arms. I began sobbing into his chest, close to his heart. "I'm so sorry, Lord! I'm so sorry!" I cried.

"I know, child. I forgive you," was his gentle reply as he held me close.

I couldn't believe what I just heard! I raised my head then and looked up into his face. I saw forgiveness there and love like none other. I then looked down at my garments. They were gleaming white! I was completely clean, and I felt that way as well!

"Oh! Thank you, Lord! Thank you!" I said. Then I went on, "Lord, I do want to follow you, but how will I know it's you?" I was concerned that I'd get confused by other people and churches. How would I know that I was following him and not trying to please others?

"You'll always know when it's me," he replied.

"Lord, if I know it's you, I'll do anything you want. Even if you want me to turn purple, I'll paint myself purple every day. I won't care what others may say as long as I know it's you." I said this because I had battled the night before about the strange ways of this church he'd brought me to and the fact that I truly thought I was saved.

Again he said, "You'll always know when it's me."

I rose and stood. I felt Christ standing behind me now, with his hands on my shoulders. I was aware of everyone else in the church taking this all in, in awe. The peace I felt was overwhelming. Brother Stewry looked at me and asked, "What happened, Patty?"

"I guess I got sanctified," was all I said.

I still didn't understand where I was spiritually, but later, I'd come to realize that I had truly been saved at that moment. That, that was when I realized my sinfulness and completely repented. All I could do then was lift my head and smile.

Everyone knew something had happened to me, yet I don't think they knew what exactly either. However, Donna came to me and hugged me. Even Sister Browning came over, praising God and gave me a gentle hug. I left the church a new creation. I knew I belonged to him. My heart was so full! Thank the Lord for his mercy and grace!

That day was March 6, 1979. I had entered into a new life with Christ. I went to as many services as I could after that. The people of the church loved me. Sister Browning helped me feel welcomed, and Brother and Sister Stewry were available to answer any question I had. I soaked in all I could like a sponge.

The very first time I opened my Bible after that wonderful night, I asked God to give me a verse to hold on to, one that I could be sure was given to me by him. As I prayed that prayer, I randomly opened my Bible to Proverbs 3:5–6. "Trust in the Lord with all thine heart and lean not unto thine own understanding. In all thy ways acknowledge him and he will direct thy paths."

I couldn't believe just how perfect that verse was for me! I needed to know that I could trust God to guide me and to know how to follow his direction and that it was his direction. This became my life verse. I call it that because it has been the one verse that has kept me firmly on the solid foundation God placed me on. Through out my walk with God, this verse has brought me hope, given me focus, and kept me on the straight and narrow. The first time I used it was just ten days after my new life began.

It was my twenty-first[st] birthday, and Walt had planned to take me to a great steakhouse, our favorite one to go out for dinner. This wasn't something we could do very often—going out to eat—but we had planned it because of the special occasion.

The restaurant was styled after the rustic western style. Its entrance was that of a long wooden-planked porch with double doors that resembled barroom doors. Inside, there were hanging lamps that looked like old-fashioned oil lamps, and the tables were covered with white cotton tablecloths and had a mason jar filled with a few wild flowers. There was a bar as you enter in through the doors, and the dinning was just off to the side.

I was so happy to be coming here. Walt and I hadn't been out on a date since I could not remember when. When we sat down at our table, the waiter asked what we'd like to drink.

I had planned on having a Singapore Sling, which was a very sweet alcoholic drink I had tried before. After all, it was my twenty-first [st] birthday, and this is what everyone we knew did on their twenty-first [st] birthday to celebrate.

As the waiter paused with his pen ready, I replied, "I'll have a cola." I just knew that it wasn't pleasing to God for me to order that drink. How? I trusted in the Lord with all my heart, and he directed my path. I can't tell you how I knew, but I did, and it humbled me to realize that. God was fulfilling his promise to me. The promise that I would always know when it's him.

"What?" questioned Walt. "You're not going to have that drink you wanted?" he asked me.

"No," I said as I slightly tilted my head as a sweet peace settled in my heart. "I just want a cola."

"Why don't you want a drink?" Walt asked me.

"God doesn't want me to," I replied.

"God doesn't want you to?" questioned Walt. "What do you mean by that?"

"I just know God doesn't want me to."

"Oh, okay," Walt replied. "Then I'll have a cola too," he told the waiter. The waiter left to fill our drink order, a bit bewildered by our conversation.

"Why do you say that?" Walt questioned me again.

"I just know God doesn't want me to drink," I told him. "Just how I know..." I shrugged my shoulders and continued, "I am sure though that he doesn't." So for my twenty-first st birthday, I gave up drinking alcohol forever.

That evening was a wonderful evening. Walter and I enjoyed each other's company for the first time in a very long time. I felt as if God was standing there smiling down on us, and he was, I'm sure.

When dinner was over, we drove home. That night, as I lay there next to Walt, I went over that night's happenings in my mind. I was so happy to have spent such a wonderful evening with my husband and just thought he never had one drop of alcohol and neither did I! This was a different kind of evening than I had ever had before.

Wow! I thought to myself lying there. "I really did know it was God." Then talking to God, I said, "How did I know it was you?" I questioned.

Then God sweetly spoke to my heart and said, "I told you, you will always know when it's me." Then I remembered the verse I had been led to, Proverbs 3:5–6, and my heart was warmed once again. "Thank you, God. Thank you for a wonderful birthday," I whispered as I fell into a peaceful sleep.

The next week, on Friday, Walt came home and asked me if I wanted to go see where he was working. "It's in the High Desert, and we will have to be looking up there for a place to live, but I want you to see it first."

"Okay," I said. "Let's drive up there tomorrow." So the next morning, we drove the sixty miles to see our future home.

We drove on the freeway, up through the Cajon Pass, until we came to the exit of Bear Valley Boulevard. As we drove up the exit, we came into the town of Victorville. Walt started to point out to me the conveniences of Victorville as he continued to maneuver through the town. There was a small strip mall, a tire shop, the San Bernardino County fair grounds, a couple of restaurants, a couple of drive-through restaurants, a decent-sized grocery store, and a couple of gas stations. We had passed a large truck stop just as we came to the crest of the overpass while still on the freeway.

"This doesn't seem too bad," I said as we started to head back home. "I don't know about living in the desert though."

"Well, it's pretty first thing in the morning, you'll see," Walt said, trying to reassure me.

"Yeah, we'll see," is all I said in reply.

The very next day, we all got in our car: Walt, me, and the girls, June and Mandy. As we drove off the exit for Hesperia, I exclaimed, "Wait a minute! Where's the town you showed me yesterday?"

Walt chuckled a little and said, "That town was Victorville. It's up at the next exit. This is Hesperia, where my work is."

"But there's nothing here!" I said in a desperate tone. Then I said under my voice, "Well, if this is what you want, God, I'll live here." Walt heard me and smiled.

As we turned onto Main Street, all I could see was desert, which consisted of sage brush, cactus, tumble weeds, a Joshua tree here and there, and dirt, lots of dry sandy dirt. As we continued, I questioned Walt, "Where are the stores, the gas stations? Where are the people?" I exclaimed. Again, Walt laughed and answered, "They're here. Just a little further up the road. You'll see."

Sure enough, we finally came to what were the businesses of Hesperia. There was a grocery store, a drive-through restaurant, a pharmacy, a gas station, and some offices. At the other end of Main Street was another business area with about the same setup.

After we drove around and Walt showed us both Hesperia and Victorville, we headed home. Later, Mom and Pop wanted to drive up with us as we looked for apartments.

We looked at a couple of apartments but didn't like any of them. Then Pop suggested looking at houses. "We might not be able to afford to rent a house," Walt said.

"I was thinking about you buying one. The interest rates are at an all time low, and the prices should be reasonable up here. Why don't we ask a realtor to help us," replied Pop.

"We can't afford to buy a house," Walt replied, a bit bewildered at his dad's suggestion.

"Let's just see first," answered Pop, and we drove to Main Street to find a realtor to help us.

In the realtor's office, Mike, who became our realtor, showed us what payment we could afford, but we'd need a down payment of $3000.00 and good credit. We told Mike that we had no down payment. "We can put up the down payment," said Pop.

"No, Pop," Walt said. "We can't let you do that."

"We want to help, and we can manage it," he replied as Mom looked up at him. We didn't know what to say.

"Well then," began Mike, "let's look at your credit." In the process of questions, it was determined that we had no established credit. "Doesn't paying rent for the last four years count?" we questioned.

"Not to a bank," replied Mike, then he went on. "But you could qualify if you had a cosigner."

"What is a cosigner?" I questioned.

"That would be having someone who has credit sign along with you on the loan. This way, the bank looks at their credit, income, etc. Then the cosigner is responsible for the payment if you should not make the payment," Mike explained.

Pop leaned over and whispered to Mom and then said, "We will cosign for them if we can do a quitclaim deed."

The realtor replied, "That can be arranged. It will have to wait six months to establish a good-paying record, and Walter's employment will be established as well. Then I'm sure the bank will let you sign it over to them. Why don't you go home and discuss this together and I'll look for some houses for you to look at tomorrow. Will that work for you?" he questioned.

"That sounds good," answered Pop.

"We'll see you then," Mike replied as he shook Pop's hand.

This was all foreign to me and Walt, so as we drove back down the hill to Mom and Pop's house, we asked, "What is a quit-claim deed?"

"It's where we cosign for you, and then in six months, we sign the deed over to you," Mom explained.

Walt went on to say, "But we don't have the down payment, Dad."

"Mom and I said we can loan it to you and you can pay us back. You need a house to raise those girls in," Pop so graciously offered. Walt and I looked at each other in amazement and drove the rest of the way in silence.

Own a house? This hadn't crossed our minds before, or at least not mine. "I don't know," I said to Walt as we sat on the back porch that evening discussing it. "This is a big undertaking."

"I know," he started and then went on to say, "but we can do it. I am making good money with the overtime, and if we rent, we're just throwing the money away. And our rent would be the same, so what's the difference?"

"The difference is, we'd owe your parents. That's a lot of money! I just don't know how we could manage a house payment and paying them back," I replied in earnest.

"Well, let's go look at some houses and see what happens. We can always say no," was his answer.

We talked with Mom and Pop and told them our concerns. They reassured us that they wanted to help us do this. So we went the next day and looked at a couple of houses and found one we all thought was a good buy and decent home.

It was an eight-hundred-and twenty five square-foot home with two bedrooms, one bath, a small eat-in kitchen, and living room. The carpet was multi-green-colored shag in the living room, multi- yellow shag in the small bedroom, and blue-white-and-green shag in the large bedroom. The largest bedroom was huge! It measured twenty by eleven, and the smallest was eleven by eleven. Each had a large closet that took up one whole wall and a large window.

The living room measured fifteen by fifteen and was paneled in dark paneling on one wall, had a front door on another wall, a sliding glass door that led out to the side/backyard, and a swamp cooler to keep the place cool during the hundred-plus-degree weather of the desert on another wall. The last wall opened up into the eight by fifteen eat-in kitchen and had a tall wall heater on it close to the entrance of the bedrooms and five by fifteen bathroom.

The kitchen had a large window on the same wall as the sliding glass door and a dining area big enough to accommodate a small table-and-chairs set. It had cheap light oak cupboards on one side with a sink and a window above the sink, which looked into the backyard. The only counter space was on either side of the sink. At the end was a place for a washer and dryer with a large cupboard above made like the rest. Then on the opposite side from the sink was room for an oven and refrigerator. We were grateful to be able to negotiate to have these appliances remain as part of the purchase since we had none of our own and could not afford to buy any.

There was an attached carport out front, a slab patio with storage behind the carport (the sliding glass doors led to this patio from the living room), and there was a fence all around the property with an allowance for parking in front of the fence. There were no sidewalks in our neighborhood. As a matter of fact, there were no sidewalks anywhere except in front of the businesses on Main Street, which was three miles away.

Our property was half an acre. There was no grass and hardly any other plants besides the Joshua tree out front on the other side of the fence and two elm trees out back. We were surrounded by open desert on all sides, with five neighbors spaced out up and down the street.

It had a chain-link fence and two large gates out front, which let you drive up the concrete driveway into the carport. Then there was the same kind of fencing separating the front yard from the back with a gate, attached to the house, next to the carport. There was even an area fenced off in the very back for livestock.

So we became the proud owners of our first house! Walt and I were as excited about the new house as the girls were. We moved in on April 1, 1979, and began a new phase in our lives.

CHAPTER 8

At first, we went down to Mom and Pop's for dinner on Sundays, so the children and I were able to continue to attend church at the Bible Covenant Church. This was a blessing as I became established in my new life in Christ. I was able to attend with Donna and became friends with another girl who had been saved a few months after me. Her name is Tammy Farmer. We would become the three musketeers of God, as some called us.

I'll never forget the first time I really felt connected to this wonderful group of Christians. Donna, Tammy, and I were singing along with the rest when the Spirit of God came upon us. We were singing "Victory in Jesus," and it hit us all at the same time.

"Victory in Jesus! My Savior forever! He sought me and he bought me with his redeeming blood. He loved me ere I knew him and all my love is due him. He plunged me to victory beneath his cleansing blood!" We jumped to our feet and sang with all we had. I was so blessed! Never had this happened to me before, but I couldn't contain myself! Neither could Donna or Tammy!

It was exhilarating and liberating all at once! I was blessed to think that ere before I knew him, he loved me! Loved *me*! That he could love someone like me was amazing to say the least. And victory he gave me! Real, honest, complete victory!

Donna, Tammy, and I just started to jump up and down and laugh and cry and hug each other! Our Savior, Jesus Christ, loved us enough to die for us while we were yet sinners! We had the victory because of him. Praise the Lord! To this day, I cannot sing that song without remembering what I experienced with my friends and Savior.

It was wonderful to be able to be with my friends and learn about God together. We were having Bible studies and prayer meetings with Sister Stewry. Then we would discuss how God was helping each of us. Both Donna and I were married to husbands who were unsaved and partook in sinful vices. Tammy was raising two children all on her own, but as she would often say "not on her own" since God came into her life.

Because Walt was needing to work on Sundays sometimes—and those he didn't work, he wanted to stay home—he said it was too far to drive every weekend, and he was right. It was sixty miles each way and an hour's drive time. So I had to tell Brother and Sister Stewry that I wouldn't be able to attend the church regularly. I was distraught by the thought of having to find another church in the upper desert.

"It'll be fine, Patty," assured Sister Stewry. "You'll still be able to visit us when you do come down and see Walt's parents, and Brother Stewry and I will look for a church up by you. You should pray and ask God to guide you to the right one. He'll help us. You'll see."

"All right. I will look, but how will I know it's right?" I asked.

"What was your verse God gave you?" she so wisely asked me.

"Trust in the Lord with all thine heart and lean not unto thine own understanding. In all thy ways acknowledge him and he will direct your path," I quoted from memory Proverbs 3:5–6.

So I started looking around for a church. "Why not go to the Catholic church again?" Walt questioned.

"Because it can't help me the way this one does. I tried it, remember? I didn't find God there," I replied.

"Well, how are you going to find one?" he questioned further.

"I'll pray about it. God will let me know where to go. He led me to the Bible Covenant and saved me there. He will guide me now," I answered.

Walt didn't know what to make of it all, but one thing for sure, he knew that there was a change in me. I wasn't so hateful, and we were really happy. So he tried to help me find a church too.

We looked in the phone book to see what kind of churches were around. There were a couple of Catholic churches, Baptist, Methodist, and Pentecostal. I had never attended any except Catholic, Calvary Chapel, and the Bible Covenant, so I didn't know about denominations. I saw one that had the word *Bible* in its name, so I asked Walt to drive me to it to go to church that Sunday. He, of course, said he would.

At the time, my dad had come to visit us and see where we were living and see our new house, not to mention to visit with his grandchildren whom he loved and missed dearly. So Dad came along for the drive. He said Walt and he would drive around and see Victorville and the area while I took June and Mandy with me to the service. Walt didn't attend church with us, and my dad was Catholic. It didn't bother me in the least. I knew I was supposed to go to church. Don't ask me how; I just knew.

When we walked into the building, I immediately noticed the songbooks were the same ones we used in the Bible Covenant Church. I also noticed it wasn't a big place and had only a cross up front behind the pulpit with a bench in front of the pulpit as well and two sides of pews. It was so similar to the Bible Covenant I thought I had found the church for me, but I soon realized that it was not.

We didn't make it to Sunday school but slipped into the back pew after a warm welcome from the pastor's wife. We read from the Bible and sang songs. Everything was as it was in the Bible Covenant church, except for a couple of things.

The women wore dresses, but their hair was cut, and they wore makeup and jewelry. It was odd that, that would bother me as I wore pants, makeup, and jewelry too, and my hair was cut. The most important thing, though, is that I did not feel the presence of God. They were very nice people, but all I could say is I didn't sense God there. After the service was over, I said good-bye to the pastor and his wife. They asked me to fill out a card with my name and address, so I did.

Dad and Walt drove up, and June, Mandy, and I climbed into the car.

"Well, we'll never go back there," I said.

"Why not?" questioned Walt.

"It's just not the same," I answered.

"They had the same songbooks and Bible, but something wasn't right."

"They had the same Bible?" Dad questioned. "Aren't they all the same?"

"No, Dad. The Catholic Bible is different than the King James. Besides, I just didn't feel God there," I answered him. I know this was a bit strange to my dad, but he just reassured me that I'd find a church. Walt joined in on that reassurance as well. Later that day, I called Sister Stewry and told her about the church.

"Just because it says Bible in the name, doesn't mean it's like ours," she said with a light chuckle. "Brother Stewry and I will come up there and have a prayer meeting and ask God to help. Is Tuesday all right, around ten?" she asked me.

"Sure!" I exclaimed excitedly. "Then you can stay for lunch afterward. Thank you so much!" They came that Tuesday, and the prayer meeting was wonderful. I knew God would help me, and he did.

The very next day, Brother Stewry called and said he found a church called the Bible Missionary Church located in Hesperia. He said he would set up a meeting with the pastor. I was so happy! God had answered my prayers! I eagerly waited to meet this new pastor.

The next day, a knock came on my door. As I opened it, I saw a well-dressed man standing there. "Good morning, Mrs. Meyer. I'm Pastor Smith. May I come in?" he questioned.

I noticed he had a Bible in his hand, and I became excited and said, "Why, yes. Please come in." Then hardly waiting for him to cross my threshold, I blurted out, "I have been looking forward to meeting you ever since Brother Stewry told me about your church. I just can't go back to that other church! They had the same songbooks and Bible, but the women wore jewelry, cut their hair, and it just wasn't the same as the Bible Covenant Church."

Then a moment of shocked silence came from Pastor Smith. Then he spoke quietly and hesitantly, "I'm sorry you feel that way. We don't feel the need to follow all those rules." Then it hit me! This was the pastor from the church I had attended in Victorville.

"Oh, I'm so sorry!" I humbly said. "I didn't remember your name and thought you were the pastor my pastor from Upland had found for me. Please forgive me. I just can't go to your church. It's not what I need," I finished.

"That's all right, Mrs. Meyer. I'm sorry we can't help you, but God bless you," he said. Then he stepped out the front door and left.

Oh my goodness! I thought. *I hope I didn't hurt his feelings. It is the way I feel, and I can't help that. Oh well, Lord, please help him.* I left the rest in God's hands.

I called the Stewrys then and informed them as to what had just transpired.

"I feel so bad!" I said.

"It's all right, Patty. God will help him," Brother Stewry said. "I was going to call you today because I was able to set up a meeting with Brother Herbert Plants. He would like to meet you at his place of employment."

"Where's that?" I questioned.

"He's the produce manager of the grocery store in Victorville. You know where that is?" he said.

"Yes, I do. When are we supposed to meet?" I asked.

"Today at noon. Does that work for you?"

"Oh, that only gives me a couple of hours, but I'll get the girls ready. Will you meet me there?"

"Well, I was hoping my wife and I could come to your house since we don't know the area. Is that all right?"

"Why sure! Come on up, and I'll have the girls ready to go when you get here." And so it was settled.

As it turned out in those two hours, Brother Stewry called me back to say they couldn't make it. "Would you mind going by yourself?" he asked, concerned about me. "I just want you to meet him before another Sunday goes by. That way, he can give you instructions on how to find the church and when the Sunday school starts as well as the services."

"I can go and meet him," I assured him.

"Good! I'll let him know you'll be there. He said to meet in front of the store. I'll tell him what you're driving and to be watching for you," he said, and then we said our good-byes.

As I drove up to the market in my 1974 white Ford Mustang hatchback, I was a bit nervous, but when Brother Plants walked up to me, I was put at ease almost immediately. He was a big man and had a big smile. As I got out of my car, he walked up to me and removed his blue store apron and reached out his hand.

"Hi! You must be Patty Meyer," he said with a big smile and a firm handshake. "I'm Herbert Plants, the pastor of the Bible Missionary Church in Hesperia. Brother Stewry called me and told me you were looking for a church to attend in the area. We'd be more than happy to have you attend our little church." He then gave me directions from Main Street to the church. We talked a bit, but he had to get back to the produce department, so I told him good-bye, that it was nice to meet him and I'd be in church for sure Sunday. He suggested I drive over and see where it was so I would know how to get there before Sunday morning.

I asked Walt if he knew where the address was. He told me where I could find Lime Street from our house. He was a bit familiar with Hesperia as his job took him all over the High Desert. So the next day, I found it easily.

As I drove up to the address, I noticed a wooden sign painted brown with the name of the church painted in yellow. I drove through the chain-link gate and parked in the small dirt parking lot on the right. I let the girls out of the car then walked up to the house that was on the property and knocked on the side door. An elderly woman around seventy-nine years old answered the door. I was surprised as I had thought this was Brother Plants's house.

"Hello," I hesitantly said. "My name is Patty Meyer."

"Oh yes! Brother Plants told me you'd be stopping by. My name is Lillie Freeman. Please do come in and sit down," she said in a very cheerful voice.

I was so young in the Lord and new to everything, but I could sense the presence of God all around that place and her. She asked if we'd like some lemonade that she had just made. I said we would, and as she went to the kitchen, I took in my surroundings.

The living room was just off the kitchen and a nice size. It was at the kitchen door that I had knocked. I had been led into the living room and sat down on the couch. The house was very clean, as I could see.

The kitchen was small but sufficient. It had a small yellow Formica table with four chairs, which were padded and covered in vinyl of the same pattern and color of the table, around it. Quite fifty-ish style. It had to be pushed up against the wall to be able to get around it. The wall had a big window, and the door had a small one at top.

There was a cupboard along the wall that was adjunct to the living room and one that had a sink on the wall opposite the large window. There was a water heater in one corner and a stove and refrigerator on the wall with the door. There were upper cupboards above each lower cupboard and yellow Formica countertops, which also matched the table, on each of those.

There were white country-style curtains with yellow daisies bordering on both the large kitchen window and door window. It was so quaint and welcoming. I fell in love with it and its occupant, whom I learned to call Sister Freeman, almost instantly.

Sister Freeman took me outside after we sat and talked a little. We walked over to what I thought was her garage. "Here it is," she said. Then she opened the door, and we walked into the church.

It was a simple setup with three rows of chairs facing a pulpit that was up on a platform. There were two wooden lowered benches for the altar set in front of the platform. There was even one bathroom in the corner.

The walls were of light-colored paneling, and the indoor/outdoor carpet was a mixture of earth tones. There was a picture of Jesus, the Shepherd, on one wall and a big square heater next to the bathroom.

Now I had been raised Catholic, and the small church in Upland was already a culture shock, but this…I knew God could meet me anywhere, but I just wasn't used to this. As she started to explain how the garage came to be the church, I then understood a little more.

Sister Freeman had come to the High Desert with her husband many years ago. As a matter of fact, I believe it was in a horse-drawn wagon! They had been holding prayer meetings and Bible studies in their home but felt the Lord prompting them to start a church. So they called around and found a denomination like the one they followed, which was Pilgrim Holiness, that would be happy to come start one in the High Desert and be happy to use their garage for the church. It was the Bible Missionary Church. They sent Brother and Sister Plants to pastor it.

Dear Sister Freeman was a true mother in Israel for me. She immediately had me join her in prayer that first day I met her, and we never stopped having prayer meetings from then on. A couple of days later, she introduced me to Sister Grace Jones and Sister Lois Whiteman. These three ladies would become my spiritual teachers throughout my young Christian walk.

Sister Jones reminded me a lot of my grandma Bissa. She was built much like my grandma and had the same sweet disposition. She took me under her wing and taught me how to pray. She would just start talking to God.

"Can I pray that way too?" I asked her.

"Certainly!" she answered.

"All you do is talk to Him?" I questioned.

"Yes, dear. God is your Heavenly Father, and He wants to talk to you," she reassured me. So as we knelt down to pray, she gently encouraged me to start. It was a bit strange for me at first, but once I started, God came.

It was the first time I ever remember praying in such a personal way. God let me know he was right there. As I prayed, I poured out my heart to him. I told him how thankful I was that he saved me. That I felt so clean and new. I just continued to pray that way, oblivious to anyone else.

After I finished, Sister Jones prayed a prayer of thanksgiving and praise. She connected with God instantly and talked to him as if he was right there. Well, he was! I loved prayer meeting and couldn't wait for the next one.

It was awesome. I had been saved only three months, but it seemed like I had always been a part of the family of God. I was blessed every day and learning in what seemed like quantum speed. My heart was full. The church services were so helpful and made my hunger for God's truth grow.

3
A TRUE FOUNDATION

"For other foundation can no man lay than that is laid,
which is Jesus Christ."

—Corinthians 3:11

CHAPTER 1

It was June 1979. We were heading up north for a surprise visit to my parents. It was their twenty-fifth ᵗʰ anniversary, and there was a surprise party planned for them. Iris and Frank Herman, their best friends, and my sisters Cathy and Barbara had planned the whole thing. Having Walt, the girls, and me come was supposed to be the extra surprise.

We all hid out in their garage, and when they had returned from a quick dinner, Cathy had them come out in some pretense. When they opened the door, they were completely surprised. It was so neat to see the look on their faces! Then Iris had Mom turn around. When she saw us, her arms flew up, and she ran over and gave me a big hug.

"Patty! Walt! When did you get here?" she hollered.

"Where are the kids?" Dad asked. He loved his grandchildren so much. "The kids are inside. We had to hide until today. We got here yesterday. We were staying at Barbara and Geoff's," I informed them.

So we brought the girls in to see Grandma and Grandpa. They were given lots of hugs and kisses while Grandpa asked them how they were doing. June had just turned four in May, and Mandy was one and a half, and I was not the same girl my parents remembered.

Back home, during our prayer meetings, I had been asking questions as to why the women of the church didn't cut their hair and why they wore dresses. The answers I was given were scriptures and an admonition from Sister Jones to read the scriptures and pray about it, to ask God to show me what he wanted me to do.

"You mean just ask him?" I questioned Sister Jones as we met for another prayer meeting at my house. "Yes, you remember the verse God gave you?" she asked me. She was referring, of course, to Proverbs 3:5–6.

"Yes," I said and then quoted, "Trust in the Lord with all your heart and lean not unto your own understanding. In all thy ways acknowledge him and he'll direct your path."

"That's right, honey." Sister Jones continued, "So ask him for guidance in this, and trust him. He'll show you what he wants you to do." So I did just that. I prayed to God and looked up the verses they gave me as to why they did what they did.

As to the question on why they didn't wear pants, the verse Sister Freeman quoted was, "The woman shall not wear that which pertaineth unto man, neither shall a man put on a woman's garment: for all that do so are abomination unto the LORD thy God" (Deuteronomy 22:5).

"You'd never see a man wear a dress would you?" she questioned.

"No, but there are men pants and women pants," I innocently replied.

"True," continued Sister Freeman. "But pants were made originally for men to work in the fields. Women didn't start wearing pants until WWII, when they started to work in factories because our men were overseas fighting the war."

"I didn't know that," I said. "I will pray about it and see what God wants me to do." So I did.

The answer to the question of why they didn't cut their hair, Sister Jones stated, "It says in 1 Corinthians 11:14–15, 'Doth not even nature itself teach you, that if a man have long hair it is a shame unto him? But if a woman have long hair; it is a glory to her; for her hair is given her for a covering.' So our hair is given to us to show we are under submission to God and our husbands, as God intended."

"Yes, and when the hippies started to rebel against authority is when men started to wear long hair. They knew it wasn't right, so that's why they did it, in rebellion," added Sister Freeman.

"Yes, but what about Jesus?" I questioned. "He had long hair."

"We don't know that for sure," answered Sister Jones. "The pictures that are painted of Jesus only show what someone thinks he looked like. No one knows for sure since they weren't there. We do know, however, that Jesus lived a life of submission to the Father, so he would never have done anything in rebellion."

"That makes sense," I said. "I'll pray for God's help in understanding these verses. I've told God I'd do anything he wanted me to, even paint myself purple, and I meant it." They giggled a bit then agreed that they'd be praying for God to show me his will. We ended that meeting with powerful prayer, and I was confident that God would show me what he wanted me to do.

I went home and looked up the scriptures and laid the whole thing before him. "Okay, God," I said, "please show me. Do you want me to stop wearing pants?"

This was big for me because I hated wearing dresses. I only owned two dresses and one skirt, and that was because for my birthday that year, Walt took me shopping for clothes and he wanted me to buy dresses.

"I like you in dresses," he stated.

"But I don't like wearing them," I retorted.

"Please, honey? You look so nice in them," he replied.

"Oh, all right," I conceded, and we made the purchase.

The thing is, this was before I was saved, but God knew what I'd need.

One dress was a light blue with short puffy sleeves in the peasant style, one was a peach-colored shirt dress with stripes and long sleeves, and another was a light-tangerine-colored peasant-style skirt with a pretty floral print and a cream-colored peasant-style long-sleeved shirt made with a crape-type material. I secretly loved them all, especially when I saw how pleased Walt was as I modeled them for him. I only pretended to be against it because I had been such a woman libber in the past, something that God was patiently changing.

"Okay, God. The scripture says that I'm not supposed to wear anything pertaining to men. I understand what Sister Freeman was saying, but there are woman pants. I can wear them, can't I?" I questioned. No answer, just a patient silence.

"What did my Word say?" Then God asked me.

"That a woman isn't supposed to wear anything that pertains to a man," I answered. I then remembered the reason for women wearing pants, which Sister Freeman gave. "Okay, God. I'll do it. I'll stop wearing pants, but you'll have to provide more dresses as I only have the three." I said, got up, and took all my pants out of my closet and drawers and threw them all in the trash. "I meant it, God, when I said I'd do anything if I knew it was you. Thank you for letting me know it's you."

What peace filled my heart at that moment! I didn't understand it then, but I knew it was God sealing my decision with his kiss of approval. It was settled, or so I thought. The test was to come when I was up north celebrating my parents twenty-fifth [th] anniversary.

Chapter 2

No, I wasn't the same girl as the last time my parents had seen me. I changed in more ways than one, and I didn't know how to talk about it to them. I didn't even know that I should. I was happy to be there and celebrating this momentous occasion with them and our family and friends.

The party was a good one. Full of family and friends. We got to connect with all of Mom and Dad's friends from my old home town of La Verne because they came to surprise Mom and Dad as well.

The days following the party, I was able to talk with Cathy and tell her the good news that I was saved! I was shocked by what she had to say about that.

"You better not say anything to Mom, Patty," Cathy told me after I joyfully shared the news of my conversion.

"What do you mean? I thought we were supposed to witness to others, and I really hope to share with Mom what God has done for me," I responded.

"Well, after that letter you wrote Mom, she was livid! She didn't take your news very well."

Right after my conversion, I had written my mother a letter explaining how happy I was since I found Jesus. "I told her that I was saved and my sins were forgiven. Why would that make her mad?" I questioned Cathy.

"I don't know. It's just the way you said it, I guess. Besides, Patty, you were already saved, and once saved, always saved!" Cathy replied heatedly.

"Obviously I wasn't, Cathy," was how I answered her.

"Yes, you were! I was there!" she answered.

"So was I!" I said. "I don't know what happened back then, Cathy, but I know I'm saved now," I answered back.

Now looking back, I can see that I really did want Christ in my life when the invitation was given at Calvary Chapel when I had attended the service with my sister. I had no idea what repentance was though. I hadn't come to see the need in my heart, yet God was faithful then to give me a hunger for him, a hunger that wouldn't be satisfied with anything but the whole truth of God's provision of salvation in Christ.

Cathy was not pleased. This saddened me as I thought she would be happy for me. I didn't realize it then but she took it personal that I had claimed that I wasn't saved before, on her watch per se. And now the joy I had was buried in fear of offending Mom and the knowledge that my testimony offended Cathy.

I was sorry they felt that way, but I knew what had happened to me. I had the witness of the Holy Spirit in my heart confirming that I was a child of God, and I didn't have that witness before. I had a peace that I didn't have before, and I had a relationship with Jesus Christ that I didn't have before. Thank God for his faithfulness to my soul!

So I spent the rest of the visit walking on pins and needles. I was constantly worried about who I'd offended next, but I prayed, and when I did, Christ sweetly came. He gave me peace and assurance that he would be with me and guide me. I was only to trust and obey.

Later that week, Cathy invited me and the girls for a swim. Walt had gone fishing with Dad and Joe. As I went to her apartment, I silently said a prayer, "Lord, help me stay true to you. Show me what you want me to do, and I'll do it, with your help." Little did I know just how much I was to be tried at this time.

As Cathy got changed into her one-piece swimsuit and she changed her kids into theirs, I became anxious. I was in my dress, and so were June and Mandy. They were in sundresses with little matching panties so they could wear those to the pool, and I told Cathy so.

"That's silly," said Cathy. "Didn't you bring suits for them?"

"No, I didn't," was my simple answer. "It's okay though. They can wear what they have on."

"Fine!" Cathy said a bit upset. "What about you?"

Oh boy, here we go! I thought. Then I answered her, "I didn't bring one either."

"Well, you can borrow my extra one. It should fit," she said, and she went to get it.

"Lord!" was all my heart could pray.

"Here. Go into the bathroom and change. We'll wait," Cathy said as she handed me the bikini and directed me to her hall bathroom.

At first, I told her I was fine and I'd just sit with my feet in the pool. I didn't need her suit.

"Oh, Patty! Just get in there and change! We don't have all day!" she ordered me. So I took the bikini and went into the bathroom to change.

As I did, I cried. I put it on and felt such shame! I felt naked! I knew that the feeling came from God's disapproval of me. He did not want me in that bikini; I was sure. So I quickly removed it and got dressed back in my dress.

"Here, Cathy. I can't wear it," I said as I handed the bikini back to her.

"What! Why not?" she asked heatedly.

"Because I felt naked in it," I honestly answered her, but I never mentioned my conviction.

"Fine! You can wear my shorts and a tank top. You'll be covered enough then!" she said.

"No, Cathy, that's fine. I'll wear my clothes. Don't worry about it. I'm fine!" I assured her. My big sister wasn't going to take no for an answer though.

"That's silly, Patty. Here! Put these on. There's nothing indecent about these!" she heatedly said as she thrust the cutoff jean shorts and white tank top into my hands.

So dejectedly, I once again entered the bathroom to change. I put on the shorts and saw that they almost came down to my knees and the tank top had wide straps and wasn't too low in front. Now I wasn't aware that these standards had become a part of me. I just knew God wasn't happy. I felt I shouldn't be wearing these either.

Cathy hollered for me to hurry up. "What's wrong now?" she questioned.

"I just don't want anyone to see me in these. What if there's guys out there?" I answered, again avoiding the fact that it was my God-given conviction.

"So what if there's guys out there. You're decent for heaven's sake! What's wrong with you? Are you worried you're fat, because you're not!" she responded.

"I just feel embarrassed, Cathy. I don't want any guys to see me in these," I stated.

"Fine! I'll go check and see if any *guys* are out there!" she said, and she went and looked down the walkway that led to the pool. "No guys. Now come on! Let's go!" she demanded. So I hesitantly came out from the bathroom. Cathy had already left with the kids in tow, so I hurried to catch up.

As I was hurrying down the walkway, I kept looking around. I didn't see anyone, and I was feeling a bit relieved. Then as we turned into the gated pool area, as Cathy opened the gate, I caught out of the side of my eye two young guys sitting on their porch, which was right in front of the pool area. They whistled at us and made a crude remark.

I panicked. "Cathy! I'm going back!" I cried to my sister.

"For Pete's sake, Patty! Just get in here! Honestly, what's gotten into you?" she questioned. Of course, she didn't know what was wrong with me. I hadn't dared tell her about the conviction God gave me. How could I? Not only was she upset about my newfound salvation, but I didn't even understand what was happening to me! So I timidly followed my big sister into the pool area.

She could tell I was nervous and said we could go down and sit in the grass away from where those guys were. So we let the kids play in the kids' pool, and we went and spread out the beach towels Cathy had gotten for us.

Cathy lay on her towel to get a tan. I lay down on my belly, trying to get as far out of view as possible. Cathy and I talked a little and then something strange yet wonderful happened.

As I lay there, leaning on my elbows, my chin in my hands, a light came down and surrounded me. I lifted my head and looked around. I could hear Cathy talking, but I couldn't see her there next to me, at least not all of her.

I could only see the bottom half of her and the grass around us. I could see the kids if I lowered my head a bit but then only saw the light when I raised it up again. It was as if the light was hovering just above the ground and was all around me.

"Lord," I whispered in my heart, "is this you?" Silence. I asked once again, "Lord, is this you?"

"Need you ask?" was the only reply.

"No, Lord, I know this is you," I stated, and I did. I sensed his omnipotence and was awed. It was as if he was hovering there on his throne in front of me, with angels on both sides.

"Lord," I continued in my heart, "you're not happy with me, are you?" Nothing. "You don't want me to wear this, do you? You don't want me to wear pants anymore, do you?"

Again the answer was, "Need you ask?"

"No, I know you're not happy with me, Lord, and I'm so sorry. Please forgive me," I prayed in my heart. Silence once again. I felt that God was so displeased with my disobedience that if I died right then, I'd miss heaven. God, of course, in his mercy was just trying me "as if by fire."

"Lord," I continued whispering in my heart, "if you'll help me make it back to the apartment, I'll put my dress back on, and I'll never put pants on again!" So I got up and told Cathy that I couldn't stand it anymore and I was going back to the apartment and change. I don't know what she thought or said. I got up immediately and ran back to her apartment.

As I got up, the presence of God followed me. I went to the apartment and directly ran into the bathroom and changed. I felt such relief! I was so happy again! I knew God was pleased and I was back in his graces. Needless to say, the battle wasn't over. Cathy could not understand, and I can't blame her because I still had not mentioned my conviction.

Within a few days, we were leaving to head back home. My brother Joe had decided to come and stay with us for a couple of weeks. My parents asked if June and Mandy could stay for a visit and they would bring them back when they came to pick Joe up. Walt said it was fine.

The day we were getting ready to leave, Mom asked me why I was wearing my dress to drive home. "Won't you be uncomfortable?" she asked. It's funny now that I think about it, but no one ever noticed that I was only wearing dresses. No one knew of my conviction because I never told anyone. I didn't dare after the talk I had with Cathy. Walt had known because I told him when it happened. He was happy because, as I had stated before, he liked me in dresses, but there was no need for him to make it known.

Anyway, as I tried to tell Mom that I was fine, again avoiding mention of my conviction, she insisted I change into some shorts. She asked if Cathy had a pair in the laundry to lend me. Cathy did her laundry at Mom's to help save money. She did, and once again, as I went to the bathroom to change, I started to cry.

"I just can't!" I cried to myself as I sat down onto the commode. "What am I going to do?" I questioned as the tears fell down my face. Then as the tears poured out, I poured out my heart to God.

"Lord, I can't tell my mom! She already hates me for my testimony. Cathy told me so! What can I do?" I cried to the Lord. Just then, Walt came in to find out what was taking me so long.

"Honey, what's wrong?" he asked as he saw I was crying.

I pulled him into the bathroom and shut the door. "I can't wear these, Walt!" I said anxiously.

"Why not?" he questioned.

"Because, remember, God doesn't want me to wear pants anymore. Not any pants, even short ones," was my reply.

"So why are you crying?" he asked as he lifted my face up in his strong hands.

"Because I know if I put these on, it'll displease God, and if I don't, Mom and Cathy will be mad," I told him.

"Well, if you feel God doesn't want you to, don't. Your mom and sister will understand, and if they don't, oh well. You're a grown woman and can make your own decisions," he wisely stated.

"You're right!" I said. "Thanks, honey. I love you."

He just smiled at me and said he loved me too.

So I put my dress back on and felt like a huge weight was lifted from my shoulders. As I came out from the bathroom, Cathy asked if the shorts didn't fit. Was that why I wasn't wearing them? "No, that's not it. I just don't want to wear them," I told her.

"Oh, go get her another pair!" demanded Mom.

"NO! Really. I'm fine," I answered.

Mom got up and rolled her eyes. She then went into the kitchen to get a drink. Cathy came over to me, guided me into the hallway, and whispered, "What is up with you?"

"Nothing," I whispered back.

"Then why don't you wear the shorts?"

"I don't want to. I'm a grown woman and can make my own decisions."

"What's going on here, Patty?" she asked more directly. "You wouldn't wear the shorts at my house and now you won't wear them here. Why?"

I thought, *Well, here goes nothing.* Then I answered, "Because God doesn't want me to."

"What do you mean God doesn't want you to?" she asked. So I testified to how God had shown me the scriptures and how he let me know he didn't want me to wear pants anymore. She was not taking that as the final word on it.

"What? So are you saying I'm a sinner for wearing pants?" she asked with a bit more volume.

"No, I didn't say that, did I?" I whispered back.

"You just said God told you it was a sin for women to wear pants!" she argued.

"I said God showed me it was sin for me. I never called you a sinner for wearing pants, did I?" I questioned. She just looked at me with disgust in her eyes. "Tell me, Cathy," I went on, "if God came to you and told you to stop wearing pants, would you?"

"He wouldn't do that," was her answer.

"How do you know? Have you ever asked him about it? Besides, if God came to you and told you to stop wearing pants, would you?"

"Well, of course I would."

"Well, it was God, and he did come to me, so I won't wear pants anymore."

"So you're judging me for wearing pants!" she said.

"No! I'm not! Are you judging me?" I retorted, and with that, the conversation came to an end.

We said our good-byes and kissed and hugged June and Mandy. "Be good girls for Grandma and Grandpa," I instructed them. They were happy to be staying, and my parents were happy to have them for a while.

"Don't worry about these guys," my dad said as he tickled Mandy's tummy. "We're going to have a great time!" June was holding Grandma's hand, and Mandy was in Grandpa's arms. They looked a bit wide-eyed but soon were smiling at my parents.

As we drove off, I could see Cathy standing there with arms folded. Walt asked me what went on during the private conversation with Cathy. I told him, and he asked why she got so upset. "I don't know. I guess she felt I was judging her, but I wasn't!"

"You mean you won't wear pants again, ever?" questioned Joe.

"No, I won't. I'm sure God told me not to, and I'll do anything he asks of me," I said, and then I testified to Joe about getting saved. It was my real first testimony besides telling Walt. Joe listened intently and was asking questions for quite a while on the trip back to our home in Hesperia.

It was a good time with my brother. We showed him around, and I invited him to go to church with me.

"Walt, you going?" Joe asked Walt.

"No," Walt replied.

"Well, you could both come and see the church I go to," I said.

"It's in a garage!" Walt said with a snicker.

"In a garage?" asked Joe. "Can you have church in a garage?"

"Of course you can. God meets us there every Sunday and Wednesday," I replied.

"Sunday and Wednesday?" Joe questioned. "Why two days?"

"We have prayer meeting on Wednesday. You guys should come and see how God meets us there," I said.

"No way. Not me!" Walt responded.

"Well, I'll just stay here with Walt. I don't go to church when I'm home either. So no hard feelings, Patty."

"None taken," I said a bit disappointed. "Lord," I silently prayed, "please save Walt. I do so want him to walk with me in this path you've brought me to. I would love to see my whole family serving you." I truly did want this more than life itself, but it was not to be for a while.

I was so happy and getting settled in the way. It was a way that was so new to me, but I was confident that this was the way God had brought me, and I wasn't turning back. Soon, my resolve would be tested yet again.

CHAPTER 3

Two weeks had passed, and my parents were due to bring June and Mandy back and pick up Joe. When the girls got out of the car, my heart sank. They were wearing short outfits!

Now I realized I hadn't told Mom that we weren't wearing pants or shorts anymore, so I couldn't blame her. "What are you wearing?" I questioned June as she ran up to me. "My new clothes Grandma got me!" she answered with a big smile.

"You only packed them dresses, so I bought them these outfits to play in. What were you thinking to pack only dresses?" Mom asked me. Well here goes nothing!

"I did that on purpose, Mom, because we only wear dresses now," I replied.

"What? Why on earth for?" she questioned.

"Because I feel that's what God wants us to do," was all I said.

"What? So you won't let them wear these?" she asked in a hurt tone.

"They can wear them, for pajamas or under their dress. I'll pray about it. They are cute."

"What do you mean pray about it? My God, Patty! They're just clothes!" Mom said, exasperated.

"I pray about everything now, Mom. I want to be sure I please God, so I ask him."

"So now you're talking to God?" Mom stated with sarcasm.

"Yes, Mom, I do, and he talks to me," I said. "Remember that letter I sent you telling you that I was saved and my sins were forgiven? Remember I told you that God had really come to me and saved me?"

"Yeah, I remember the letter, and boy, did it make me mad!"

"Mad? Why?"

"Because who do you think you are that God would come to you?"

"Well, he did. I'm no one, and that's the point. He came to me to show me the way he wants me to go."

"Well, I think that sounds as if you're a bit loony. Besides, what's wrong with the Catholic church? Are you saying I'm damned, Patty? Are you?" Mom said, a bit upset.

"Now, Mary Ann, let's just let it go. We're here to visit the kids and see their house," Dad interrupted. So the matter was dropped for the time being, and we went on with our visit.

Later that day, Mom and I went to the store to pick up a few things for dinner and to snack on. We talked a bit about the clothes thing, and I reassured Mom that the outfits were fine. That I'd use them and the girls looked cute in them.

"I have to say though, Mom, that I will do whatever God wants me to do. I can't go back to what I was, and I just want to please him," I was saying as we drove into my driveway.

"Well, I'm telling you, Patty, that this will ruin your marriage!" Mom said. Then with tears in her eyes, she said, "Don't think I don't know what's going on in your marriage. I wasn't fooled by that black-eye story you gave us when you lived in La Verne. If it wasn't for your father, I would've brought you home right then. I called your father and told him the lie you gave me and told him I didn't believe it for one minute. He said if you didn't feel the need to leave, then we weren't to get involved. But then he said if it ever happens again, he would come and take you home!"

"Mom! That was a long time ago," I said.

"Not that long ago," she replied. She was referring to a time when June was about one and a half and we had a party at our two-bedroom apartment in La Verne.

We had our apartment full of people. Even my sister and her husband, Mark, was there along with Walt's brother, Billy. We all had way too much to drink. Walt had passed out on our bed, and finally, everyone else was asleep somewhere on the floor.

I climbed into bed, and as I did, Walt started to slide off the other side. He was laughing, and so was I. We both were drunk, but him more than I. Suddenly, Walt jumped up and started pounding my face with his fist! I saw stars, literally.

As he continued to pound my face, I was able to get my feet under his chest and pushed him off me. I proceeded to cuss at him and put up my fist. "If you want to fight," I screamed at him, "then come on!"

He was laughing again and spun around to face me. Suddenly, he stopped laughing. His eyes became wide, and he said, "Oh, Patty! What happened?" as he staggered over to me.

"What happened!" I screamed back. "You did, you idiot!"

He just said, "I did that?" as he reached for my face. "Wow!"

I pushed him away and started throwing punches at him. I screamed that I hated him. Then I left him there and went to the bathroom. As I turned on the light and looked into the mirror, I saw that the whole right side of my face was black and blue, and my eye was swollen shut already. My whole face hurt, so I turned on the cold water and splashed the cool water on my face. As the coolness washed over my face, I calmed down. I then grabbed a washcloth, placed it in the cold running water to soak, and then put it over my swollen eye and cheek.

Cathy had woken up and stuck her head in and asked what we were fighting about. I told her that Walt had hit me, and she said I probably deserved it. Wow! How could she say that? No one else was awake. "Go back to bed," she said as she went to lie back down in June's bedroom.

So holding the washcloth to my face, I walked into our bedroom. Walt had fallen asleep. *How could he after what he did!* I angrily thought. I was so mad that I just left the apartment.

I went to the car and realized I didn't have the keys. I saw a new pack of cigarettes in the back window. *Probably Mark's,* I thought. Neither Walt nor I smoked, and we had picked up Cathy, Mark, and little Mark for the party. "Well, I need a smoke!" I told myself, and I took the pack and found the lighter lying next to it and took it as well.

I started to walk down the dimly lit street from our apartment. I had done this many times before, whenever we fought, which was often. I used to take June with me, threatening Walt that we were never coming back. Then I'd sit in a tree hidden from sight and watch Walt drive all around looking for us. I'd eventually go home. Where else could I go? I had no one to go to. I did this because I was so immature and felt lost. I just couldn't cope.

Yet this time, I was furious! "How dare he hit me like that? I hadn't done anything to deserve that! What was Cathy talking about?" I stopped walking to light up a cigarette, and I started to smoke.

My hand was shaking as I lit the cigarette. "Look at me! Look at what he's done to me!" I just kept talking to myself.

I'd light a cigarette and draw on it real hard. The first one didn't even make me cough, so I quickly lit another. Then it was one right after another as I walked the darkened streets. It was way past midnight somewhere in the early morning, hours before dawn.

As I continued down D Street, I walked past the church where the tree was that I would hide out in. As I turned and looked at the tree, I said, "God, is there any hope for us?" not really thinking God heard me. No, I wasn't stopping here this time. I knew Walt was passed out, so he wouldn't be looking for me.

I'll just go get a hot cocoa, I thought and headed down D Street toward our local doughnut shop. As I walked, I continued to light up and smoke one cigarette after another. When I came close to the doughnut shop, I saw police cars out front.

I couldn't go in there. They'd ask questions about my face, and Walt will get arrested. So I turned around and headed back home. As I walked the darkened streets home, I had time to think.

Walt was so drunk he really didn't know what he was doing. This was quite obvious. I was still angry, but I couldn't hate him. I finished the pack of cigarettes just as I came to our apartment. "Wow! I guess I was upset. I smoked the whole pack!" I said as I entered the apartment. I went straight to our bedroom, fell into bed, and was soon fast asleep.

In a few hours, when Walt woke up, saw my face, and was sober, he asked me what happened. "How did you get a black eye?" he asked me.

"You!" was all I said.

"What? I wouldn't do that to you," he said, bewildered.

"Well, you did!" And I went on to explain just how. After I finished telling him what he had done, he begged me to forgive him. He promised he'd never lay a hand on me again, and he kept that promise. But now, what were we going to tell everyone?

"What are we going to tell your mom, Patty? She's coming for a visit! Your dad will kill me! They'll make you leave me!" exclaimed Walt. So I came up with a story.

"We will just say that since Billy had to lay down on our bed [which he did for a while], that I put our shower curtain down just in case he threw up. Then I say I slipped on the plastic and fell into the bed post and hit my eye.

As we told everyone our lie the next day as they gasped at my swollen face and black eye, a friend named Cheryl said, "If he hit her, she deserved it, I'm sure."

"Probably," chimed in Cathy.

Wow! I thought. *They have no reason to say that, and they don't even know what went on, so how could they say that?*

No one believed this story, except Walt's mom. Billy got in trouble for it. Even though my parents didn't believe it, there wasn't anything they could do. I wouldn't leave Walt. We had so many problems, but I still loved him and he me.

That love was fine but not enough to make our lives happy. This was just one more event in the many hurtful events that we both caused in our rocky marriage.

Maybe it was that prayer, asking God if there was any hope for us, that was the beginning of God bringing an answer. It wasn't too long after that when we had moved to Northern California and found some relief but still not the answer to our problems. God knew the answer. It was that we needed him.

Even though neither of us was raised to understand that God longed for a relationship with us, God still moved in our lives to bring it about, at least in my life even though my mother could not see that it was God at the time.

So here we sat with Mom in tears and her telling me my marriage would never make it. "If you don't change back, Patty," she said in a pleading voice, "you'll lose Walt! Your marriage will fail!"

"Oh, Mom," I tenderly replied. "You have no idea where my marriage was and where it is now. Without God, I wouldn't be here."

"Well, if you don't change back, you'll never see me here again!" she said with finality.

What did she just say? How was I to answer that? I knew exactly how as the Spirit sweetly settled in my heart. I felt pity for Mom. I couldn't blame her. After all, our marriage wasn't the best, and I hadn't witnessed to her before, except for the letter. As far as she knew, I was entering some kind of weird cult. She couldn't understand what it was to have a relationship with God. In the Catholic church, you were taught that, that was impossible. That you could only connect with God through the church.

"Well, Mom," I said, "I'm sorry to hear you say that. I love you so very much, but I love God more, and I can't give up what he's given to me. I can't go back. I won't."

"Then I won't be coming back here to see you. It hurts me to say that, Patty," she spoke in a choked voice.

"I know, Mom. I wish you felt differently, but I understand. I hope you can come to understand my position some day. You know I love you though, right?"

"Yes, and I love you, but I can't budge on this. I worry for your marriage. What does Walt say about all this?" she asked.

"He's fine with it. Like I said, you have no idea where our marriage was before. We're happy now, and Walt's fine." So we went back into the house and after a couple of days, waved good-bye to my parents as they drove away. My mother was true to her word. She didn't come back again, not at least until God made a way.

I realize that it was difficult for Mom to understand my convictions. After all, this was completely different from the way she had raised me. I hated that my convictions made others feel like I was passing judgment on them, especially my family. I had friends who didn't go to my church, and they didn't have a problem with me being different. I couldn't understand why my family had a problem. This was what God was doing, and I was just obeying his will for me.

The dress was just one conviction. God had led me to a holiness church, he had saved me in a holiness church, and he had a direct hand in leading me to this holiness church. I knew it was God, and I wasn't going to go back. I had passed the test and was now ready to settle all the convictions God wanted me to learn, strange as they even may have seemed to me back then.

CHAPTER 4

The next thing God had convicted me on was the makeup. I never wore a lot, but I was wearing a bit more than when Walt and I first started dating. He hated me wearing so much, but I didn't care. I felt I looked better with it, and I still did what I wanted. I noticed though, that not only did the older ladies in the church not wear makeup but neither did Tammy or Donna, so I asked why.

"Makeup is only mentioned in the Bible as a description for prostitutes," Donna told me.

"No. Really?" I asked. So she showed me in the Bible where it was giving a description of a prostitute, and sure enough, there it was. It said that they painted their eyes and lips to lure the men to their beds.

"Wow! I didn't know that," I said. "But I don't wear it for that reason! I don't hardly wear any."

"Well, it does say that. That's why I don't wear it anymore," Donna replied.

I pondered that for a while. I even asked Sister Freeman and Sister Lois about it during one of our prayer meetings. (Sister Jones had passed away while I was up north visiting my parents. I wholeheartedly missed her.) The ladies shared the same scriptures with me as Donna had. I explained that I didn't see the wrong in it but that I'd pray about it. They agreed to pray with me about it too.

So one day, shortly after that prayer meeting, I was at the mirror putting on my makeup. As I started to apply the mascara, God spoke to my heart.

"What are you doing?" he questioned me.

"I'm putting on my makeup," I answered back.

"Why?" was all he said next.

"Because I want to look good," I replied.

"Don't you like what I've created?" came back the question.

"Really? No!" I honestly stated.

I wasn't trying to be disrespectful, just honest. God knew that, and he understood. Not only did he understand the situation, he understood how to help me see the truth. So he was patient in his dealing with me.

"I made you the way I want you to be. Why would you try to change my creation?" he reasoned with me.

"I just don't think I'm that pretty," I replied. Then silence.

I had come to know that, that silence was one of love and not anger. One of patience and mercy. So I put down the mascara wand and submitted to the will of God. "I don't like my looks, but I am yours, so I'll never wear makeup again, Lord. I love you," I said out loud.

"I love you too," came the reply in my heart.

Peace! Such sweet peace! I had come to realize that the feeling was one of assurance, of approval, and of love. I realized that it came from the throne of God every time I submitted to his will. To submit was all I could do to show my love for him who gave so much for me! I couldn't do otherwise.

That same peace and assurance of approval was there when I submitted to no longer cutting my hair, it was there when I submitted to no longer wearing pants, and now it was here when I submitted to no longer wearing makeup.

Why wouldn't I want to do his will? It only brings peace! Hardships may come because of my choice to follow God's will, but the peace was always there.

Once, I learned in my Bible readings that we are to make restitutions when we steal something. It seemed that even the sermons at church were dealing with it. God was so faithful to help me see his light!

During that time of enlightenment, Walt and I were invited to an anniversary party of one of my old neighbors', the Galas. We were able to bring the girls with us too. I was so looking forward to it because my parents came from Rohnert Park and would be there as well.

While there, the Spirit talked to my soul. "Remember how you stole makeup from Ginger?" he asked me in my heart.

"Yes, that's right!" I said. Ginger was a neighbor I had babysat for, and when I would be leaving on a date from her house (my sister would take over for me), I would use her makeup.

"Well," continued the Spirit, "what do you think you should do?" So I slipped into one of the bedrooms to pray about it.

"I don't know," I said.

"What does my Word say?" he whispered to me.

"That we're to make restitution for it. To pay it back," I replied.

"That's right," he whispered again.

"But I have no idea how much I took. It was just a little at a time. What am I supposed to pay back?" I questioned. Immediately, the amount of $10.00 came to my mind.

"I don't have that on me," I stated.

"Write a check," replied the Spirit. So I went and got my purse. As I did, Walt asked me where I had been and why was I getting my purse. So I explained to him about how God had been dealing with me and that I had to write Ginger a check for $10.00. He just smiled at me and said, "Okay. Is that all? You're sure?"

"Yes, I have to do this, and this is how much," I replied.

So I wrote the check and went to find Ginger. "Ginger," I started to say as I stopped her, "I need to give this to you. I would use your makeup when I was babysitting. I'm a Christian now, and God told me that this is what I owed to you. It was stealing, and I owe this to you. I just hope you can forgive me." I handed her the check.

She just looked at me bewildered at first. "Please! Take it! I owe it to you, and I am so sorry! Please forgive me!" I said with misty eyes.

"All right. Thank you, and I do forgive you," she kindly said.

"Thank you!" I said as the weight of guilt was lifted from my shoulders.

I then took June and Mandy over to the grass in the backyard and sat down with them. We played a couple of games, and as we did, I sensed angels surrounding us. It seemed as if they were singing a joyous melody, or was it just my heart? It was both, I'm sure. My heart was so light, and I felt such happiness. On and off that day, I caught Ginger watching me and pondering the happenings in her mind, but it did not matter if she understood. I knew beyond any doubt that I had done exactly what God had wanted me to and I had his blessing. What more could I want?

Another conviction came about when the church asked me to stop wearing my wedding ring while I taught Sunday school.

I had been attending the Bible Missionary Church in Hesperia for about five months and was asked if I would like to teach the youngest Sunday school class. I was excited to do so. I learned a lot while preparing lessons. After all, I was just a babe in Christ. So we were on the same learning level.

Anyway, after a few weeks of teaching, one Sunday after service, Brother Plants came and asked me if I wouldn't mind removing my wedding ring while at church. He told me he didn't mind me wearing it but other members of the church did.

"Why?" I asked.

"Because it's in our manual not to wear jewelry," Brother Plants stated kind of hesitantly. "It's fine if you wear it anywhere else, but since it's in our manual, I have to ask you to remove it during church. You understand, don't you?" he asked anxiously.

"Yes, I understand, but I don't want to be a hypocrite. If the kids see that I don't wear it here but do at home, what will they think?" I answered. I had started bringing a couple of other children from the neighborhood to church with me and my girls. I was concerned that they would see me not wearing my ring at church and then wearing it at home, the store, etc. This would look hypocritical. So I asked, "Why don't you wear jewelry?"

Brother Plants proceeded to show me the scriptures that the manual used about not adorning yourselves in golden apparel. I told him I'd pray about it, and I did.

As I prayed that night and the next day, I looked up the scripture and found that it was talking about jewelry. "But this is my wedding ring. I won't wear any other jewelry, but I can't take this off even if it means I have to stop teaching Sunday school," I said as I spoke with God.

"But they need your help to teach. I want you to teach," God told to me.

"But this is my wedding ring!" I replied.

"Why do you wear it?" God asked me.

"Because I'm married," I replied.

"But why do you wear it?"

"Like I said, because I'm married and others will know I'm married by me wearing it."

"Shouldn't they know you're married by the way you act?"

"Yes."

"Then why do you wear it?"

"Because Walt wants me to."

"Do you love him more than me?"

"No!"

So I removed the ring from off my finger. I didn't know how Walt would react, but I knew I had to do this to please God. Three days later, Walt noticed I wasn't wearing it.

"Where's your wedding ring!" he asked as he grabbed my hand.

"It's in the nightstand. I haven't been wearing it for three days now," I told him.

"Why?" So I told him what God had asked me to do. "I love you, honey, but I love God more."

"Well, I'm going to take my ring off then!" he said heatedly.

"Go ahead. I know I can trust you," I said.

"But how are guys going to know you're married if you're not wearing a wedding ring?" he asked.

"That's what I asked God, and do you know what he told me?" I questioned Walt.

"What?" he said reservedly.

"He told me others should know I'm married by how I act. Let me ask you something, Walt. Before I was saved and I wore my ring, could you trust me?" I asked with a tilt of the head and a gleam in my eye. I knew the answer to that.

"No," came the reply.

Then looking him straight in the eye with deep love, I asked, "Can you trust me now that I'm saved?"

"Yes," he whispered. "I do."

From that point on, neither of us ever wore our wedding rings again.

Even as I'm writing this, I realize that with each and every conviction, God made sure Walt was part of the deciding factor. Not that I made the decision because of Walt, but God saw that Walt had to be part of the equation. After all, we were married. We are one flesh, even if I didn't understand that yet. God is so good!

These were the foundations of my obedience to God. It was important because I had much to learn, and just as God called Abraham out from among his people to go to a promised land, God was calling me. He was establishing the foundation of my faith, and he was preparing to build on this foundation. I had so much more to learn, but first, I had to learn the truth.

I was eager to learn all that God had for me. I went to every service. If the church doors were open, I was there. I went to every Bible study at Sister Freeman's and became very close to her. She took me out, going door to door, passing out gospel tracts, and witnessing to others about the Lord.

We had weekly Bible clubs. This was when I'd bring the kids from the neighborhood to Sister Freeman's, and she'd tell them a Bible story with flannelgraph and have songs and serve cookies afterward. The kids came to love this. Sister Freeman even had me attend a child evangelism course to learn how to reach the children for Christ, and later, I had the Bible club meetings at my house with upwards to fifteen in attendance right there in my living room.

I couldn't get enough. The more I learned, the more it became a part of my life. I lived and breathed for God. Yet no matter what I said or did, I couldn't get Walt interested, and this became harder to bear. I just couldn't understand why he didn't want to become a Christian. Who wouldn't? I didn't realize that it was God who calls us to repentance. It just wasn't Walt's time yet.

CHAPTER 5

It was shortly after we had moved to Hesperia, and as I was walking in all the light God gave me, when Lois asked if I ever had my girls dedicated. "What's that?" I asked her. She explained that in dedicating the baby, I was giving them back to God. That I was promising to raise the baby in holiness and the fear and admiration of the Lord.

"Oh," I said, "like baptizing them. Yeah, I did that in the Catholic church."

"No, not quite," replied Lois. "It's more than just saying you're going to raise them this way. It's also that you are giving back to God what he's given you." This was a no-brainer for me. If it was what I was supposed to do for my children, I would do it. So Lois suggested I talk with Brother Plants about it, and I did.

After he went over the scriptures of giving your children to the Lord, to raise them in the admonition of the Lord, I was thoroughly convinced this was God's will. I needed to make that statement. That I was going to raise my children to love God and to follow him and that the old-fashioned holiness way was the way to do it. After all, God had brought me this way and shown me it was his way for me. Why would I train my children to go any other? Also, I was giving June and Mandy back to God. They were his to begin with. I came to realize that he had just loaned them to me.

"Well, talk it over with Walt," Brother Plants told me.

"Why?" I asked. "He doesn't have a say in their spiritual life."

You see, once during our first summer in Hesperia, Walt had let June and Mandy run around without a shirt and play in the water. I came home and was upset. "How could you let them run around like that?" I had questioned.

"Why? What's wrong with that?" he asked.

"They're indecent!" I answered.

"They're just little girls! They're only one and a half and four. They can't be indecent," he replied.

"I don't want them growing up thinking it's okay!" I shouted. "If it's okay now, what makes it not okay later?"

"That's silly. Besides, they're my kids too, and I have a say in the way they're raised," he rightfully stated. Yet Walt never went to church, and he hardly had anything to do with us since he started at the construction company.

Since all the guys drank beer after a hard day's work in the hot sun, Walt's drinking was getting worse. I had, had enough of his drinking and also of everyone telling me I was wrong to be taking the Christian stand I was taking. No one else was making an effort to follow Christ and surely not Walt.

So when Walt made that statement, I arrogantly said, "You have no say in the way these kids are raised! Not until you start going to church!" As if going to church would change things, but I was so ignorant!

Now Brother Plants was saying I needed to talk to Walt about dedicating the girls to Christ. I didn't think I needed his approval, and I surely didn't think he'd even care. Was I wrong.

Brother Plants wisely insisted that I talk to Walt. He helped me see that Walt should at least have a chance to come if he chose to. "Okay, I'll tell him, but he probably won't come, and I'm doing it if he wants to or not," I said.

"That's fine, but do talk with him. After all, he is their father," Brother Plants said. So I agreed to talk to Walt.

I went home and told him that I was going to have the girls dedicated the next Sunday. "What's that?" he asked. So I explained what it was. Walt said he wanted to be there.

"You do? Why?" I asked, completely surprised.

"Because they're my kids too," he said.

"Yeah, but you don't go to church, so why do you care?"

"I may not go to church, but I know that this is the way that we should raise them."

"The way we should raise them? What do you have to do with it?"

How arrogant and disrespectful could I be? These were his children, and God was obviously moving in his heart. What was I thinking responding that way? It hurt Walt terribly, and he hung his head.

"I may not go to church with you," Walt started, "but I can see a change in you, and I know it's right. Can I please come?" he asked me in a subdued tone of voice.

Can he come? He was asking my approval! I looked into his eyes and saw a glimmer of hope in them. "Of course you can come. I just didn't think you'd care one way or the other," I said.

"Well, I do care, and I want to be there for them."

"Okay. So you'll come to church with us on Sunday?" I asked.

"Yes, and let's call Mom and Dad and let them know too. They may want to come," he excitedly said in a lighter spirit.

"Why would they want to come?" I asked. I hadn't thought any further than getting the girls dedicated. Now Walt was wanting to be there and have his parents there too? He even said we could have a barbeque afterward to celebrate.

"It's like a baptism, right?" he asked. "When we had the girls baptized Catholic, your parents came. I'm sure Mom and Dad would want to come." So we called them and let them know what was happening. They decided not to come, and Walt was a bit disappointed, but I was used to everyone treating my walk with God as unimportant and a bother, so I wasn't that disappointed; besides, nothing would deter me from doing this.

When that Sunday rolled around, I dressed the girls in their prettiest dresses. These were dresses that a dear saint of God made. Her name was Sister Potts, and she was our own Dorcas.

She worked for a company that made very expensive and pretty dresses for little girls. When there were scraps, she was permitted to take them home for her own personal use. She made hundreds, if not thousands, of little girls' tiered dresses with ruffles and lace and gave them to church families and missionary families all over the world. We were so grateful, and I am positive she has a crown full of jewels in heaven!

Anyway, the girls were wearing the pretty pink floral dresses, and I had curled their hair. They looked so cute! Walt was beaming with pride, and I was in awe of how God was once again having Walt there for an important spiritual step in my life and the lives of our children.

As Brother Plants started the ceremony, Walt and I brought June and Mandy up to the altar. Brother Plants spoke of how important it was to dedicate the children to God. That in so doing, we both were willingly giving them back to God and acknowledging that they belonged to him. That we were promising to raise them in the way of holiness and to help them find a true relationship with God. He then prayed a beautiful prayer for all of us and anointed June and Mandy with anointing oil.

The presence of God filled our little sanctuary! It was beautiful and awe-inspiring. Walt and I both had tears of joy and hearts full of peace. I knew then that Walt was truly part of this wonderful time and he was completely surrendered to God's will for his family. This was encouraging, yet he wouldn't surrender his life to God. That would prove to be a difficult situation for me to accept, especially as life went on.

His drinking was getting to be a big problem. On July 4, 1979, we went to his parents' for a family picnic. Well, there was plenty of good food, family time, and lots of beer. Walt drank all day long. After the fireworks and more drinking, he was finally ready to head home.

We had purchased a 1968 Jeep truck from a neighbor and had driven that there. The girls sat behind the seats on the drive home and were curled up on pillows and blankets, asleep.

Walt's mom had asked me to drive home. She knew Walt had too much to drink, but Walt wouldn't have it. So as we drove home, I prayed and prayed fervently.

As we drove down the freeway, we hadn't gotten too far when I realized Walt wasn't able to handle this drive home. I begged him to pull over and let me drive.

"No! I can do it!" he slurred. Not only was he drunk, but he was tired because of the late hour. He started to fall asleep at the wheel. "Walt!" I shouted.

"Huh? What?" he said, annoyed at me.

"You're falling asleep at the wheel! Please let me drive!" I begged.

"Nah! I'm fine. I'll handle it," he said and continued to drive down the freeway. When we came to the ramp of the intersection to the interstate that led up the Cajon Pass toward home, he started to fall asleep again.

"Lord! Help us! Please get him to let me drive or help him be able to drive," I pleaded with God. Walt jerked his head up just then as we were headed too close to the railing since he was driving up the ramp. "Whoa!" he said. "I guess I better let you drive." So he pulled over and gave me the keys.

"Are you sure you're not too tired?" he asked. He knew I usually slept on long drives, and this was an hour drive, not to mention the lateness of the hour. "I can do it. I'm tired but not as bad off as you. Really, honey," I said, "I can do it."

"Well, wake me up if you get too tired. I should be fine if I sleep a little bit," he replied. So I promised him I would, but I didn't think he was in any shape to drive, so I prayed.

"God," I started praying in my heart as I drove onto the interstate, "I'm so tired too, but I can't let Walt drive! He's so tired and has had so much to drink today. Please help me stay awake." I drove just a short distance when my head and eyes grew heavy, so I opened the window.

Walt jerked up and asked if I was okay. "I'm fine," I replied.

"I just need some air to help me stay awake."

"Okay, but you better let me drive if you can't," he said as he fell back to sleep. I sat straight and took in the cool night air.

"God," I continued to pray, "I need your help. If I can't do this, Walt will take over and I'm afraid he'll get us killed!"

"Trust me," God whispered into my heart.

"Okay, I will," I replied in my thoughts and continued to drive with a bit more ease.

Suddenly, I was jerking my head back up. "God!" I started again with earnest. "I can't go to sleep! You've got to help me! Should I wake him up?"

"Just relax," God replied.

"Relax? I can't relax! I have to drive home," I answered.

"I know. Trust me. You do trust me, don't you?" God questioned me. Then I remembered Proverbs 3:5, "Trust in the Lord with all thine heart and lean not unto thine own understanding."

"Yes, I do trust you, Lord," I said and continued down the road.

Suddenly, I was jerking my head up. I had only driven a few miles since I took over, and now twice, I was jerking my head up from falling to sleep. I was scared and didn't know what to do.

"You're not trusting me," God whispered to me.

"I can't fall asleep!" I replied.

"You must trust me. You can trust me," God said.

"Okay, I will," I replied. "I do trust you, Lord. I do." I relaxed and felt a deep peace fill me. We were just coming up to the long incline of the pass, and I took a deep breath.

The next thing I knew, I was driving off the interstate onto the exit for Hesperia. *What happened?* I thought. "How did we get here?" When I realized that God had miraculously helped me make it to our exit, without an accident, I started to say out load, "Praise the Lord! Thank you, Jesus! Thank you!"

"What?" Walt said as he woke up to my praises. "I said, 'Praise the Lord!'" I told him.

"Why?" he questioned me. Then I told him what happened. "What? You said you'd wake me up if you got tired," he said.

"I know, and I'm sorry. I knew you were just too tired, and I wanted to do it, but when I couldn't, God told me to trust him. So I did, and he drove us home!" I told him with such joy in my voice. Walt just laughed then told me to let him take over now. "I can drive home now. We are almost home, and besides, I'm too excited to sleep now!" I replied. As I drove down Main Street onto Balsam then home, my heart sang a new song. One of awe and praise to the God who is able to do exceedingly, abundantly above all that we ask or think.

Maybe having this experience is one of the reasons Walt wanted to be a part of the dedicating of his two girls. I don't know. I do know he loved the girls and me; he loved God even but wasn't ready to surrender to him. I think God just wasn't real enough to him, but God is more than real to me. He is my everything. My Savior!

CHAPTER 6

It was less than one year later when I found out I was expecting our third child. I was excited as this baby would start its life in a home where Christ was followed and his ways were taught. I was still such a babe in Christ that it seemed like my children and I were growing up together. Now I was to have one who I could start fresh with. This baby wouldn't have to suffer all my failures like June and Mandy did. At least that's what I thought. What I didn't realize is that as children learn through trial and error, so do Christians. I wouldn't come to realize this truth until many years and heartaches later.

It was January 16, 1981. I had started labor pains and was needing to get to the hospital. I had called Walt, and he was finally home. I could smell beer on his breath, and I was upset yet didn't have time to think about it.

My friend, Denise Stultz, was there to watch the girls for me. I had been babysitting her two children, Debbie and Sean, who were the same ages as June and Mandy respectfully, for a while, and we had became close friends.

As Walt started to head for the hospital, he asked me how far apart my contractions were. "They're less than two minutes apart!" I anxiously replied. "Hurry and don't stop for red lights if you can help it!"

We already had two deliveries that had gone quick, and this one was no different. Actually, it was going faster, but thankfully, my doctor was aware of my quick deliveries and had instructed the staff that when I said I needed to push, they were to get me into the delivery room immediately. Soon after reaching the hospital, I was in the delivery room with Walt by my side welcoming Crystal Rose into the world. This time, I was ready with a name.

As always, Walter Lewis was the boy's name, but we had chosen the girl's name with the help of my brother Joe, who was now living in the High Desert as well. Joe had said he always liked the name Crystal. "Crystal, I like it! If it's a girl, let's name the baby Crystal Rose," I told Walt.

"Hey! That's the name I chose," Joe said.

"Yeah, but I like it too. I love the real crystal, and I love roses, so it's perfect!" I said.

Then Walt said, "Crystal Rose. That's real pretty. And my sister was Rose. The one who was killed. I'd like to name her after my sister."

So when they asked us what her name was, we didn't hesitate. "Crystal Rose," we said.

"Well, please spell that. There's a lot of ways to spell Crystal," the nurse said.

"Just like the stuff," I said. "C-R-Y-S-T-A-L and then R-O-S-E."

"That's a pretty name," the nurse said.

"My delicate little rose," I said, then I kissed her on her forehead as I held this new little daughter in my arms. "She's so pretty, honey!" Walt said as he stroked her head. She had dark hair and blue eyes. She would look straight at you. You could tell she would be inquisitive. She was just so sweet! Walt then bent down and kissed her on the top of her head. He was no longer the least bit drunk, and he was mystified by yet another little daughter.

Walt has wanted a daughter from the beginning. I, on the other hand, had hoped for a boy, at least once. God, though, blessed us with three beautiful girls, and Walt couldn't be happier, and honestly, neither could I.

Soon, we were released from the hospital and was able to go home. June and Mandy were so excited to have a baby in the home. They were wonderful big sisters. I also reminded Walt that when I had decided to get the girls dedicated, I had promised God that the first Sunday after the birth of the baby, I would have the new baby dedicated. I didn't want to wait, and he agreed. Again, his parents would not come. They were not pleased with my choice of churches either.

Mom Meyer had told me that when she was young, that her family went to a church like the one I was going to. She said that at one service, they were taking up an offering for some need in the church. When the plate was passed to her father, he put some money in. Mom then remembered the pastor saying, "Brother De Vors, we know you just got paid and have more than that to give." So her father put his whole pay into the offering, and they went hungry.

Then she remembered at another time, she and her sister came to church in the only nice dresses they had. They were a bit worn and had been let down as far as it could go. They reached to just below their knees. Well, the pastor came up to her father and said that if the girls couldn't dress decently, they shouldn't come. So her father gathered them together and left and never came back.

I reassured Mom that this church wasn't like that. I reminded her that I wore pants when I first came and no one was offended. I also reminded her that my convictions came from God and would not change for anyone.

"Well, these are Walter's girls too. What about him?" she questioned.

"When he decides to take his stand for God, then he can have a say. Until then, I will do what I know God wants," I replied. Maybe Mom thought my religious choices were the cause of our problems. I don't know, but his drinking had become a big problem.

Because of Walt's drinking becoming a problem, bitterness was creeping into my heart. Neither of our families was supportive of my choice to follow Christ, and Walt wasn't taking the way with me. Yet the Lord was so good to me to give me supportive friends—friends in and out of church.

I needed this support team as Walters drinking became worse. As it did I began to harden my heart and as the bitterness grew, so did our problems.

4
LIFE AFTER DEATH

"Jesus said unto her, I am the resurrection, and the life: he that believeth in me, though he were dead, yet shall he live: and whosoever liveth and believeth in me shall never die. Believest thou this? She saith unto him, Yea Lord: I believe that you are the Christ, the Son of God, which should come into the world."

—John 11:25

CHAPTER 1

The first strike that hardened my heart was ten months after Crystal was born. I had found out I was expecting again. It was the middle of November of the same year, and I had gone back to the OB who delivered Crystal. I had missed two menstrual cycles and thought I had better get it checked out. I didn't plan it to be that soon, but I was pregnant once again. It was unexpected but welcomed.

Denise and I had developed a special friendship. She watched the girls for me when I went to the doctor. I told her I was a bit worried as Crystal wouldn't even be two when the baby was born.

"Crystal is just a baby herself! I don't want her to feel neglected," I said anxiously.

"She won't!" Denise reassured. "Besides, Debbie and Sean are about the same months apart as Crystal and the baby will be. They turned out fine, and I did it on my own." Then she told me not to worry, that she would be there to help me when I needed it.

"Thanks, Denise. I guess it'll be fine." Then I laughed and added, "It'll have to be! I'm having a baby!" Then Denise and I hugged each other. I was truly excited about this baby now.

I went home and told Walt. He was a bit surprised but seemed fine with it. He too said, "It has to be okay. What else can it be? Then he anxiously stated, I just don't know how we're going to make it."

"I don't either, Walt," I said, "but I do know we've always made it no matter how hard. Besides, I know God will make a way." With that, we settled in for the duration.

It was now December of 1981. The doctor told me I was about three months along when I saw him in mid-November. I was so excited because I felt the first kick!

"Walt!" I said after Walt had come home one evening. "I felt the baby kick!"

"Isn't it a bit early?" he questioned.

"No. I'm three months along. I should be feeling it kick. I was just wondering when I would."

"Wow! Are you that far along already?"

"Yep! Less than six months to go!" I said, smiling.

He smiled back then said, "Ready or not!"

Well, Walt's drinking was getting worse. There was seldom a time he came home sober, but I kept going to church and prayer meetings, finding new light in my walk with God and doing my best to follow it. I would get discouraged about the drinking but was learning to lean on God.

It had become a normal thing for us to have people over for a barbecue on Friday nights, and in the process, there would be lots of beer drinking among the guys. The women would visit, while the kids played. It was before one of those Friday nights that I started spotting earlier in the day.

I had spotted once—earlier that week—but this time I felt slight cramping. I told Denise, and she took me to the doctor. I had just seen him a couple of weeks earlier. I explained the situation to the doctor who then examined me. In his office, he told me I was probably miscarrying.

"What? Is there anything I can do?" I anxiously asked him.

"Well, if there is a chance that this pregnancy will stay viable, you'll need to go home and put your feet up. No lifting of any kind. Not even your children. No vacuuming, etc. Just get rest. But, if the cramping increases or the bleeding doesn't stop by morning, you come back here and I'll reexamine you. If it worsens, you will need to go to the hospital." Then he paused. "Now don't get your hopes up. I said 'if' there's a chance."

"I understand, doctor," I replied. "I'll do what you said. I don't want to lose the baby! Besides, I serve God who is able to save my baby!" He just looked at me, bewildered. He was from India, and I don't think he believed in the one true God. Then I got dressed and went to the waiting room. I told Denise all the doctor said and his instructions.

"Well, let's get you home, and I'll help out with the kids," Denise so kindly offered. For the rest of the day, Denise helped me around the house, and we planned for the guys to barbecue. That way, I wouldn't have to get up. When Walt got home, I filled him in on my situation and told him that was why we had planned a barbecue.

Walt liked the idea of a barbecue. "Great! Rick's here to see Bills dirt bike." he said as his breath reeked with the smell of beer. We were storing Bill's bike which he had purchased from Walt's friend, Jim Plough. I had already asked Denise and John to come over and now more were coming.

"Walt!" I started. "I'm trying to prevent myself from miscarrying! I can't be having a bunch of people here!"

"You said Denise and John were coming!" he replied.

"Yes but that's because the doctor said I have to keep my feet up and I can't be running around. Denise offered to help me." I said anxiously.

"Good! She'll be here so there's no worry then." Did he really not realize the situation I was facing?

"Fine, but I'm not doing anything for your friends. I have to keep my feet up if I'm going to keep this baby!" I said sternly.

"Fine!" Walt yelled back.

So the crowd showed up, and it wasn't too bad at first. Then Jim Plough showed up and was happy to see his old bike. I was able to keep my feet up, but as the night wore on, guys were coming in and out of the house. They all had already begun drinking and were becoming steadily drunk. Some would stop and ask how I was, but Walt never did. He was too busy with his buddies out in the garage. Then they began riding the dirt bike.

PATRICIA MEYER

It was around 6 p.m. The cramping seemed to be subsiding, so Denise and John went home. I told her not to worry.

"Thanks, Denise," I said. "But I know John needs to get home. Thanks for all your help."

"You promise you'll keep your feet up?" she asked me.

"Yes. I promise! Now go home and I'll call you tomorrow morning."

So they left. The kids were in bed, and I continued to lie on the couch with my feet up.

Suddenly, Walt came rushing into the living room from outside!

"Patty! Jim wrecked on his motorcycle! Come on and help him!" he shouted at me as he stumbled to the couch I was laying on.

"I can't, Walt! I'm trying to not loose this baby! If it's that bad, call an ambulance!" I anxiously replied. "Oh! How bad is it?"

"It's bad! He was doing a wheelie and crashed! He hit his head and he's not moving!" he said. "Come on, Patty, he needs help!" What should I do? I didn't want to loose this baby!

"Walt, I could loose this baby!" I told him. He didn't even hear me.

"Come on! Get up!" he shouted at me as he grabbed me and pulled me off the couch. He was so drunk he could hardly walk straight. It was at that moment that I hardened my heart. I got up.

"Fine! Show me where he is," I said angrily. Then I felt compassion and ran out with Walt to check on Jim.

I got next to him and crouched down on the pavement. Then I saw his head was bleeding and he was unconscious.

"Someone call for an ambulance! No one move him! He might have a broken neck," I ordered. Grandma Debbie; our neighbor and Denise's mom; had come out of her house to see what had happened. She ran back into her house and called the police. They immediately dispatched the EMTs. Walt grabbed my arm, and I had to struggle not to fall.

Walt!" I shouted. "Calm down. The ambulance is on its way."

| 176 |

We waited for what seemed like and hour, but in reality it was only a few minutes. After evaluating the situation the EMTs loaded Jim into the ambulance. The police were asking questions for their report. I told them what I knew, then informed them of my situation.

"Well, you shouldn't be out here." one of the officers said. "Go put your feet up." I just shook my head and wearily walked back into the house in a fog. "I don't want to loose this baby, God but I had to help Jim! Please keep your hand on the baby, Lord, please!" I pleaded silently with God.

I laid down on the couch; once again; while Walt was filling the police in on the details of the accident. No one was arrested, but they told everyone to head home and get off the streets.

So finally everyone left, and we went to bed. I was able to get back to putting my feet up, but my heart was anxious.

The next day, Walt was working on his oldest brother, Don, in-law's house. Don lived in Duarte, which was ninety minutes away. They were doing some home improvements and were paying Walt for his help. We needed the money. I told him I was still bleeding, and the cramping was back.

"I have to go. I need to get this done," was all Walt said.

I need you too, but I don't count! I thought bitterly. He left early that morning.

The bleeding was getting worse, so I called Denise. "It's a lot more!" I told her anxiously. "I'll be over soon. Get off your feet!" she ordered, and I did. As the day wore on, I started to cramp up bad. Denise had me call Walt and tell him he needed to get home. He said he was almost done and would be headed home shortly.

"I have to clean up here, then I'll be on my way," he assured me.

The cramping never subsided, and Denise became insistent that I get to the hospital.

"You need to at least call the doctor, Patty," Denise said. She was very concerned about my cramping.

"The cramps seem more like contractions." They were and they were getting very regular. So we called the doctor, and he told us to go to the hospital right away.

"I don't want to go without Walt!" I anxiously said.

"Well, you better call and see if he's left. If not, we have to go anyways," she said. So I called Walt's brothers house. My sister-in-law, Debbie, said Walt had left already.

"How long ago?" I questioned. Then I went on to explain the situation. "The doctor said to get to the hospital."

"Oh Patty, if we knew we would have told Walt to skip today!" she replied.

"That's okay, Deb. There's nothing anyone could do, and Walt really wanted to get it done as he doesn't have much more time," I said, then she informed me that Walt had just left a few minutes ago.

It was now over two hours after I called him, and he wasn't home yet.

"Patty, you've got to go now!" Denise said. "I'll take you."

I could always count on Denise, but who would watch the kids? How will Walt know where I am? "Mom can watch them until Walt gets here. Then she can send him to the hospital," Denise offered.

"Okay. I guess since he's not here," I sadly replied.

So Grandma Debbie rushed over as Denise helped me out of the house towards her car. Just as she was helping me in the car, Walt drove up.

"Where have you been?" I shouted. "I needed you!"

"Where are you going?"

"I called over two hours ago! It's a ninety-minute drive!"

"We stopped at mom and pops for some lunch." he replied.

"Well, I'm losing the baby!"

"I called mom before I called Donnie's to get their phone number! Why didn't she tell you? Well, I just told her I needed you to get home. I never mentioned the miscarriage." I cried out as tears came and another pain floored me.

"Stop arguing and get her to the hospital now!" Denise demanded. Finally, Walt helps me into his El Camino and gets in the other side.

"Thanks, Denise,"

"That's fine. I'll watch the kids. Just get her to the hospital pronto!"

"Where were you?"

"I'm sorry," he said. "I just didn't know."

"I know but I needed you, and as usual you weren't here! Now I'm losing the baby! Does it matter to you?"

"Yes! It matters to me!" Walt said as he reached out and took my hand. "I'm sorry! I love you, honey! We're almost to the hospital."

I cried and cried while waiting for the doctor. I told Walt I wanted this baby.

"I know, honey. I know." It was all he said as he kissed my hand. Finally, the doctor came in. After examining me, he told me I was definitely miscarrying. I just cried some more as Walt continued to hold my hand.

We lost our little baby on December 7, 1981. I was so depressed about it. It seemed like it was no big deal to everyone, but I had lost my baby! I realize now that no one else had a physical connection to it but me. Maybe that's why it seemed like no one else missed her so.

Yes, it was a girl. I prayed and asked God to let me know, and he did. I named her Sarah. We call her that to this day. After all, in God's word it says, "Before I formed thee in the belly I knew thee" (Jeremiah 1:5a); So God knew what my baby was, and he was the only one who could understand my loss.

It was difficult to come out of the depression that followed, but Denise was so kind and helped me remember that I was blessed with three beautiful daughters. Lois and Sister Freeman helped me pray. Sister Freeman seemed to truly understand. She had miscarried herself and understood my dismay.

On the Sunday morning after my miscarriage and after a beautiful service where I went to the altar to pray for comfort, I asked Brother Plants if we could have a service for the baby.

"Kind of a funeral?" I asked. I soon realized it was a difficult place for me to have put him, but he was very kind and compassionate.

"I understand what you must be going through, Patty. I just don't think we can do a funeral. We can have a service in memory of the baby," he kindly offered.

Then I sadly withdrew my request. I realized that I was putting him in a difficult place. Besides, no one else including Walt, seemed to care about the loss as much as I do. I told this to Brother Plants.

"It's not that they don't care, Patty," he said. "It's just that there wasn't the connection with the baby as there was with you. You were connected at conception, no one else was." That explanation truly helped me!

How could anyone else understand? They couldn't! "They sympathize with you," he went on. "They even feel sad, especially Walt, but they just can't experience the loss the same as you."

Well, maybe others felt sad. But not Walt! The thought was fleeting as the memory of how he cried with me in the hospital came to mind. Once again, I was unaware of the bitterness I was letting into my heart.

"Thank you, Brother Plants," I said. "I understand, and it won't be necessary anymore. I know the baby is with the Lord and I will see her again."

"Her?" he questioned.

"Yeah, I prayed and asked God what it was. After all, doesn't the Bible say that he knows the baby from conception? So after I lost the baby, I just had to know what it was. I asked him to let me know and he did."

He then smiled and praised my faith.

I didn't deserve any praise. My heart was hardening, but God's mercy was extended to me once again. How glorious is his grace!

How endless is his mercy! I was now able to move on and leave Sarah with God. After all, I still had three beautiful girls with me! And Crystal was just a baby herself! As I drove home from church that Sunday morning, I was finally able to praise the Lord once again and the girls, and I sang "Jesus Loves Me" all the way home.

CHAPTER 2

On January 16, 1982, we celebrated Crystal's first birthday. Since I was now working at Baskin Robbins and Janet Powell; the owner and new friend; was teaching me to decorate cakes, I decorated her birthday cake. We had Denise and her kids there, along with Walt's family and my brother Joe and his girlfriend, Kendle. It was a fun time. Once again, joy was in my heart and in our lives.

It was that same month that we found out that Kendle and Joe were expecting. Joe was so excited! Kendle was a bit scared. I was able to talk to her as we had become very close. She had even taught Mandy as a student teacher. She was already loved in our family!

She had come to me before she told Joe. I think she was trying to get my perspective and support. She had learned that I had been in the same predicament myself and could see that it had worked out for Walt and me.

"Are you planning to have the baby?" I asked. She said some people had suggested she get an abortion.

"But how do you feel?" I asked, earnestly praying in my heart that she'd say she wanted to keep the baby.

"I want to keep it, but what do you think Joe will say?" she asked me.

I understood her feelings of insecurity very well. That was how I had felt when I was expecting June Ann. I told her this and reassured her that Joe was crazy about her!

"He is constantly asking me if I think you will leave him! He thinks you're too smart and too beautiful for him. That you will get tired of him and leave!" I said with a smile and a chuckle.

"Really?" she replied. "That's how I feel about him."

"Well, you're both crazy! Crazy about each other that is!" Then we both laughed and went on to discuss when and how she would tell Joe.

It was February 13, 1982 when Joe and Kendle married. I helped plan their wedding and was more than happy to do so, as I felt cheated out of mine. I even made their wedding cake and prepared the food for the reception with the gracious help of Janet and Denise. My parents came, but you could tell it was a hard time for them.

The ceremony was officiated by Brother Plants in a bigger church, one where Brother Plants had known the pastor. It wasn't a Catholic church, and Brother Plants wasn't a priest. These things made it hard for my parents, but they supported Joe and Kendle and were encouraged in their decision to get married.

I was truly happy for them from the beginning and became increasingly thankful that there would be a baby born in our family around the time I would have had Sarah. Yes, life had entered our home once again.

Then in May, I missed a cycle. It was after celebrating June's seventh birthday that I realized the month had passed without any cycle for me. Could it be? Could I be pregnant again? I didn't wait two months this time. As soon as I realized the absence, I went to the doctor.

To my joy, I was expecting again! It was so soon after the miscarriage that Denise was concerned.

"Be sure you keep up with your vitamins, Patty," she offered. "Your body hasn't had enough time to heal. They say you should wait two years between pregnancies before getting pregnant. That way your body has rebuilt itself and is healthy enough to carry to term."

"I know," I replied. "I think that's why God has allowed me to be pregnant. I really wasn't trying to get pregnant." I really believed it was from the Lord. To help heal my broken heart and it did.

Back then, you didn't get sonograms and couldn't determine the sex. So once again, we had the boy's name ready. It would be, Walter Lewis Meyer, after Walt. Since I figured this would be our last pregnancy, and said so, Walt suggested naming the baby after me if it was a girl. Now we had two names ready. Walter Lewis if it was a boy and Patricia Ann if it was a girl. Soon we would find out which it would be.

CHAPTER 3

It was during this same year that my cousin, Kevin Kassel, moved in with us. He was a reporter/photographer and needed a place to stay for a while. He was a blessing in disguise! He was so much fun to have around. Walt found him annoying at times, but I think Walt was a bit jealous because we turned to Kevin for fun, something we could not turn to Walt for. That was because Walt was lost in his own world of work and drinking. Nothing else seemed to matter.

Walt has always been a hard worker. He never missed a day of work, even if he was sick. He truly was, and is, a good provider. It's just that he felt that was enough. Or maybe it was that he felt it was all he could do. After all, I had drifted further and further from him. I became lost in my Christian walk as he became lost in his drinking. We each found "companionship" in both since we couldn't find it in each other.

It became a daily battle to want to stay married to him, and I'm sure he felt the same way about me. When Kevin came, it made me even more aware of just how far apart Walt and I were becoming, and again, maybe Walt could sense the distance as well.

We had three beautiful daughters, and we both loved each of them with all our heart, but we were losing love for one another. Thank God another child was on its way. Children are a blessing from God, and it was with each child that our lives together became more meaningful. As a matter of fact, the girls were the only meaningful thing in our marriage.

Now it was January 12, 1983. I had known that the baby may come before Crystals second birthday, so I planned ahead and had things bought and Denise on hand to help. She had become very attached to Crystal and was happy to help. She was also the designated babysitter for when I went into the hospital since June and Mandy were attending the same school as her kids, Debbie and Sean. Yet, since Kevin was now there, the plan was for him to watch the kids if I went into labor during the evening. And so it was that evening of January 12 that I would go into labor.

We had just finished dinner, and I was cleaning up the dishes, when I felt the first contraction. An hour passed and my contractions were getting stronger and a bit closer. I decided I had better get the kids in bed, and hopefully asleep, before I had to leave for the hospital. Walt had come home quite drunk and had already passed out on our bed. As I kissed the last of the girls on the head and said good-night with admonishment to go to sleep, I was nearly floored with yet another strong contraction.

I realized I would need to get to the hospital right away. My labors had all been short ones, and the doctor was different from the one I had with Crystal. I didn't think he'd take me too seriously when I said I would go fast. I went into our bedroom and tried to get Walt up.

"Walt!" I started. "We have to go!"

"Go where?" he slurred.

"Go to the hospital, you idiot! I'm about to have this baby!" I retorted! I realized that Kevin might hear me, so I changed my tone of voice and once again, tried to get Walt up. "Honey! Please!" Then another hard contraction. It had only been two minutes since the last. I had to get going.

"Kevin," I started as I went to the living room clinging to the walls. "Can you take me to the hospital?"

"What! Why?" he asked anxiously.

"Because I'm in labor and my contractions are too close!" I answered him.

"No, no, no!" he said. "Where's Walt?"

"I tried to get him up but I can't, and I can't wait any more!"

"Well, I'll get him up. Just watch me," he said and he went to the bedroom and lifted Walt off the bed.

"Hey, Walt! Buddy! Your wife is in labor and needs you to take her to the hospital so, you better sober up quick because I am not doing it!" he said. I was having another contraction and was leaning on the hall wall. June and Mandy were wondering what was going on and seemed a bit anxious.

"Mommy is going to have the baby tonight, girls," I told them. "Kevin is getting daddy for me, and we are going to go to the hospital. Kevin will be here for you so, you be good girls and go to sleep."

"Okay mommy," they replied.

"I love you girls," I told them.

"Love you too, Mommy." June replied.

"Me too!" chimed in Mandy. Crystal was sound asleep.

"Please Lord! Please help Walt to sober up." I silently prayed. Just then, Walt falls into the room and says, "Are you sure you're in labor? It's not time yet."

I wasn't due for another week, and I usually ran late, but ready or not, this baby was coming. That's exactly what I told Walt. Suddenly he seemed to sober up.

"Okay! Kevin, can we use your car? Mine is almost out of gas, and I don't want to run out on the way," he said as he helped me to the front door.

"Sure! Just get going before the baby gets here!" Kevin answered, reaching into his pocket for the keys and tossing them to Walt. Finally, we were on our way.

Kevin owned his car out right, but the car was a 1972 brown Ford Pinto. It had a hole rusted through the floor, and it wasn't able to go very fast. Or at least I didn't think, so I instructed Walt. "Hurry! The baby's coming!"

"I'm going as fast as the car will go, honey!" he said as he came to a stop at an intersection. "Don't stop! Just check for traffic and keep going!" I hollered through yet another contraction.

Well, my new doctor wasn't even on call that evening. His associate was called in as I got there. I guess they knew of my short labor history, for when I told them how far apart the pains were and how long they were lasting, they didn't hesitate to call the doctor. They got me ready, and as everyone left the room, Walt came in and I told him I needed to use the restroom.

Walt helped me up and into the rest room. I sat there for what seemed like only a minute when the nurse came into the room.

"Where's your wife?" I heard her ask Walt.

"She had to use the restroom," he answered.

"What?" exclaimed the nurse. "Get back into the bed!" she ordered me as she opened the door.

"But I have to go!" I said.

She then grabbed my arm, pulled me up, and ordered me to get up in the bed.

"You don't have to go! You're having the baby!" she explained as she examined me.

"Get her in delivery, stat!" she shouted. "I can see the head crowning!" So the nurses attending me pushed me into the delivery room. As they did, they instructed me not to push.

"But I can't help it. Here it comes again!" I cried. I arched my back, desperately fighting the urge to push!

Quickly, I was helped onto the delivery table and abandoned! All the nurses scrambled to get things ready. The nurse at the station was on the phone.

"The doctor's on his way!" she shouted to me and Walt. Walt had followed at my side. I was squeezing the life out of his hand, trying once again to fight back the urge to push.

I looked at Walt and said as sweat fell from my face, "I can't wait any more!"

"But you have to, honey!" Walt replied with complete fear on his face. "She can't wait anymore!" he shouted out as yet another urge to push angrily surfaced.

"The doctors here! He's changing out of his coat now!" the nurse replied.

"Walt!" I shouted between clinched teeth. "Get down there! The baby's coming! I don't want it to drop to the floor!"

"But I can't deliver the baby!" he said as he looked into my eyes. I saw his fear and he saw mine.

"Someone has to do this!" I said as I felt the baby's head slipping. Just then the nurse looked up.

"Oh my god!" she cried out. "I can see the head! The whole head!"

Bravely Walt got up and began to make his way quickly around the table. At exactly the same time, the doctor, who had one arm in his suit coat and one in his white coat, came into the delivery room and caught the baby!

"Thank you, God!" I cried as Walt once again took up his place at my side. Instructions were flying as to what was immediately needed for the doctor and baby. All I could do was cry. That was the scariest thing I had ever gone through! Walt felt the same way, I'm sure.

Finally, after a few minutes, the doctor announced that it was a girl! I laid my head down and gave a deep sigh of relief as my head was spinning. *Thank you, Lord, for keeping her safe*, I thought to myself.

"A girl!" Walt said with a relieved smile on his face.

"She's beautiful!" said the nurse. "What is her name going to be?" She securely wrapped her up in a receiving blanket. "Speedy Gonzalez?" she jokingly asked as she laid her in my arms. "You gave us a run for our money little lady."

She had dark hair, and lots of it! Her eyes were deep blue, and she just cuddled into your arms. She was so precious!

"We're going to name her Patricia Ann," Walt said.

"No," I slowly replied as I looked on the face of this precious little blessing.

"But that's what we decided. If it was a boy, we'd name him after me and if it was a girl we'd name her after you, remember?" Walt said, a bit bewildered.

"I know, but she just isn't a Patricia. Look at her! It just doesn't fit her." I snuggled close to her.

Walt looked down at his new baby girl. "You're right! It doesn't fit her. What are we going to name her then?"

"I don't know yet. It'll come to us."

Then the nurse said, "Well, it better be soon because they won't let you take her home without a name, you know."

"We'll figure it out. I just can't see her as Patricia," I said.

"Okay. We'll think about it tonight," Walt replied as he bent down and kissed the baby on the head.

"I love you," he whispered to her. "I love you both." He kissed me and left the room.

Well, it was the next day and we still hadn't thought of a name. I was allowed to stay one more day, considering the nature of my delivery. Also, the doctor knew I had three other children at home and would need any amount of rest I could get.

That night, they brought me the baby. Walt came to visit us with the girls. June and Mandy were wide-eyed as they looked on the baby. Crystal reached out for her and wanted to play! It was so cute to see the girls love on their new little sister.

"What's her name, Daddy?" Mandy asked Walt.

"Patty!" said June. "Just like Mommy's!"

"Well, no, honey. We aren't naming her Patty," I said.

"Why not?" Mandy asked as June looked bewildered.

"It doesn't fit her."

"What are we going to call her then?" asked June.

"I don't know just yet. We'll figure it out." Then they all gave me and the baby a kiss and said good-bye.

The next morning, the nurse brought the baby and asked me for a name. "You're going home today, and if this baby doesn't have a name, she will stay. We have to have a name for the record," she informed me. So I held our nameless sweet baby in my arms to think.

"Dawn!" I said out loud as I looked on her little face. "That doesn't quite fit. What are we to name you?" Just then, Walt called the room.

"Hi, honey. How are you doing?" he asked.

"Fine. I have the baby right here in my arms," I said and smiled down at her. "Honey, they said I will be discharged today."

"Good!" Walt interrupted.

"Yes, but they won't let us take the baby without a name. They have to have one for their records. What do you want to name her? I can't think of one." I was a bit exasperated.

"How about Loretta?"questioned Walt.

"Loretta?" I looked on her precious face. "That's it!" I said excitedly. "It fits her! Where did you get that name?"

"That's my grandmother's name. She called last night to congratulate us. I like the name. Now you pick out the middle name."he said.

"Okay. How about Dawn? I was thinking about that name, but it didn't fit for a first name. Loretta Dawn. How does that sound?"

"Loretta Dawn. Beautiful! I like it!" he replied.

So, as I hung up the phone, I looked on my new little girl and whispered, "Loretta Dawn. Beautiful!" Then I kissed her and smiled as the nurse entered the room.

Yes, it was a beautiful name. It fit her perfectly. God knew who she is and always had her name chosen. We were just a bit slow in figuring it out. I thank God for all our beautiful girls. Each one is special in her own way and each one's birth gave our marriage a reason to go on. Truly, children are a blessing from God.

CHAPTER 4

It was 1983, and we now had four daughters ranging in age from newborn to seven. Life had settled into its usual routine, but I was becoming more and more unsatisfied. I didn't realize it yet because I had just had a beautiful baby girl.

I was continuing to go to church on Sundays and prayer meetings on Wednesday, bringing the kids with me. I took care of the house and fed my family but tried to find happiness any way I could.

I ran around with my girl friends and Kevin, who was still living with us, would join us once in awhile. Kevin constantly found ways to have fun. After all, this was his new home, and he was exploring all the things to do.

Walt continued to go to work and support us financially, but that was the only support he gave. Every night, he'd come home drunk. Maybe it was somewhat because he thought we were running around all day while he was hard at work. Whatever the reason, Walt was becoming more and more distant. That may be so, but I couldn't continue sitting around doing nothing with the kids. We were having a good time, and Walt wasn't a part of it. Sadly, we were falling out of love and fast.

My attitude became very disrespectful toward Walt. I once decided to go visit Terri Reedy; another friend, from my neighborhood, whom I became close to. Terri and her family had moved north to Techachapi in Central California. So I made up my mind to go, without permission from Walt. I didn't respect him, so why would I ask. I did, however, tell him.

"I'm going to take the kids and go see Terri tomorrow. I might stay a couple of days," I told Walt when he came home that Thursday evening.

"No, you're not," he replied back.

"I wasn't asking your permission, Walt," I said with a smirk on my face. "I'm telling you I'm going. I just figured you should know since I'll be taking the kids."

"You're not going!" he shouted at me, something that was a normal for us.

I leaned my face ever so close to his and said with such hatred, between clenched teeth, "I am not asking you. I'm telling you. I'm going!"

"Well, you can't take the kids!" he said hotly.

I closed my eyes and took a deep breath. I could sense God's disapproval, so I calmly said, "Look. The kids are on school break, and I am taking them and going up to see Terri." I was not giving in. I would not ask, and I certainly would not obey him. I pushed the thought that I might be displeasing God out of my head and hardened my heart even more.

I ended up going even though Walt had forbidden me to go. *Forbid me! We'd see about that!* I thought to myself as we drove out of Hesperia toward Tehachapi. "He doesn't care about us! He only cares about his stupid beer! I'm done trying, Lord!" I cried out as tears fell down my face.

Soon, we had to stop for gas. We were somewhere out in the desert, at a small gas station, just before the turnoff toward Tehachapi. I had to change Loretta's diaper, so I opened the trunk of our 1963 Ford Galaxy and lay her in it to have enough room.

After I finished changing her, I lifted her into my arms and closed the trunk. I put her back in the baby car seat and turned to go get my purse so I could pay for the gas.

As I went to get my purse from the front seat, I realized I had put it down in the trunk while changing the baby's diaper. I then leaned in to get the keys out of the ignition, and to my dismay, they weren't there. I had put them in the trunk too! What was I going to do? I couldn't even pay to get any gas.

Frantically, I tried to think of what to do. I couldn't call Terri because her phone number was in my purse! "God!" I now cried out to him, "what can I do? Please help me!"

"Call Walt," is all he said.

That was not what I wanted to do. I paced back and forth. "What am I going to do?" I cried to myself. I sat back behind the wheel. I wasn't going anywhere. Even if someone was nice enough to give me money to get gas, my keys were in the trunk.

"Call Walt," God's voice sternly spoke to my heart again.

"Fine! I'll call Walt! I guess I have to!" I said bitterly. I had no other choice. It was getting late, and we were at least an hour from home. So I finally went into the gas station and asked if I could use their phone.

I called Walt and explained the situation. "Why did you go?" is all he could say.

"Just come and get us! It's going to be dark soon!" I said. Silence. "Please, Walt. Please!"

"I'm just trying to figure out where you are and how to come and get you."

"Drive your car!" I said a bit hastily.

"But it's almost out of gas, and I don't have enough money to get more," he said.

"Probably spent it on beer," I said.

"No! You took it!" he returned, and he was right.

"Oh, okay. Just ask Kevin to bring you or to borrow some money for gas."

"I'll see if he can bring me, but where are you again?" he asked.

"I took the way you went the last time we drove to the Devil's Punch Bowl and we stopped at this gas station," I told him and then I gave him the names of the cross roads we were on. The Devil's Punch Bowl is a state park where we had gone as a family not too long ago.

"Oh, you mean the place we stopped for beer?" he asked.

"When *you* stopped for beer," I reminded. "Yeah. The same place where the woman asked for your ID." That memory brought a smile to my face.

"Okay, I'll get there as soon as I can," he said.

"Thanks. We'll be waiting in the car." Then I went back to wait.

As I climbed back behind the wheel, I was thinking of that time the woman had asked for Walt's ID. It was back in May or June, and Walt just had to stop and buy a six pack. I had asked if we could stop and get a Styrofoam cooler and some drinks. The park was in the desert, and I felt we would need the drinks. Walt agreed and proceeded toward the beer section of the store. I didn't like that he was getting beer and driving, but I didn't want to fight with him.

I came up behind Walt as he was pulling out his wallet. I was carrying Loretta, and the other three girls were running around. I started to laugh. "Are you getting carded?" I asked. Walt just looked at me. Then I looked up to the woman. "All these kids are his! That one's eight!" I told her with a smile on my face as I pointed toward June. "That would make him twelve when she was born if he wasn't twenty-one. He's near thirty!" She wasn't smiling and took his ID. I just kept laughing as I rounded up the girls and headed for the car.

The memory had softened my attitude somewhat, but I was exhausted. I then leaned my weary head against the steering wheel. This was going to be a long wait! The girls were behaving pretty well. They had coloring books and toys. I even took them out of the car for a bit to let them run around, but that didn't last too long with traffic picking up. It was past four, and even out in the desert, people were headed home from their jobs.

We all were in the car, and time was dragging on. "Where is he?" I said out loud. Then in my thought, I said, "God, I'm sorry.

I shouldn't have come. I know he didn't want me to, but I really wanted to see Terri!"

"No, you didn't," God said back.

"Well, it would've been nice to see her, but yeah, you're right. I just wanted out of there. I just can't take his drinking anymore God!"

Then the usual battle began in my heart. The Holy Spirit showed me that my attitude was wrong. I finally admitted to that truth. "But he's a drunk! He doesn't love me!" I said in my defense. But God wasn't responding to that.

"Patty, you were wrong. He's your husband," God said.

"Yeah, but isn't he suppose to show me he loves me? Sure he works hard all day, but I don't need his money! I need him!" I cried out. The battle continued until I came to the place of repentance.

"Lord, I'm sorry. I just can't do this anymore!" I said. Finally, I submitted to God's will. "I guess I'll have to stay married if that's what you want. Please then, Lord, forgive me, and please get him saved! Please, Lord. Please."

When Walt drove up, it was getting dark. He was able to get the trunk opened and get my purse and keys out. Kevin offered to buy the kids some crackers. That was good since we hadn't eaten since we ate the lunch I had packed. I then went in and called Terri and explained what had happened. She was relieved as she had been worried.

"Well, God didn't let me get too far. I really wanted to come, but I guess he didn't want me to. I'll see you some other time. Thanks, Terri, and thank Ed too for me."

"We're just glad you're all right. I'll be praying for you guys. God's ways are best," she told me. Then we said our good-byes, and I was now on my way home.

It was a long drive back. Kevin had offered to take June and Mandy with him, but Walt said no. Then Kevin said he'd head out to see his friend in a nearby town since he was out this way.

"Thanks, Kevin. I appreciate the help," I said.

"That's okay, cousin," he replied. "Just get an extra key and maybe put it under the fender or somewhere so you don't get locked out again."

"This wouldn't have happened if she'd just stayed home," Walt said, a bit annoyed.

"Yeah, but it's always better safe than sorry," Kevin said as he got in his car and then drove off.

"I guess he's right. I could maybe make a place to put one," Walt said to me.

"Could you?" I asked. "This could have happened anywhere, but you're right. God showed me just how wrong I was." I then told him how things played out and how I saw that God worked it out the way he did to get my attention.

The purse and key being locked in the trunk was his plan, his intervention for my disobedience. I normally would never do that—take my purse with me or the keys. Why I decided to change the baby in the trunk was a question I couldn't answer. I really could have, and usually would have, changed her on the front seat.

My heart now a bit softened, I told Walt, "Thank you for coming."

"Well, what else could I do?" he said.

"You could have said no. You wouldn't come."

"No, I couldn't. I couldn't have left you stranded. Besides, you had my kids," he said, almost in an angry tone.

"See, God!" I said in my heart. "He doesn't love me. It's his kids, our kids, that matter. Why do you want me to stay with him?" I asked as the hardening resumed in my heart. "Well, stop and get our kids something to eat. It's been a long day, and they're hungry," I retorted.

"No! I just want to get back home!" he shouted at me. The distance between us grew even greater as we drove home in silence. Even the girls kept quiet all the way home.

CHAPTER 5

We were headed into our ninth year of marriage in 1983. It was getting more and more difficult to want to stay married. Walt was drinking nonstop now. Nothing I did seemed to help. I continued to try to be the best Christian I could. Not only did I need to for my children, but my deepest prayer was that Walt would get saved and serve God with me.

Donna and Rick had moved up in the desert, and that was good, for a while. We each had our good friends to keep us happy. We got together for barbecues all the time with everyone. There was Rick and Donna and their three boys, Denise and John and their two kids, Joe and Kendle with little Joey, Kevin and us with our four girls. Once in a while, Tammy would come up to visit with her two kids.

I had the church family as well, which Donna and Tammy were part of. Donna, Tammy and I would have Bible study as we loved to dive into the scriptures. Also I'd meet with Lois and Sister Freeman for prayer meetings during the day once a week. Sister Freeman also had Bible club for the kids once a week.

It was enough to help us carry on, but my heart was growing more and more bitter toward Walt and his drinking. Eventually, his own friends would see that the drinking was getting out of hand.

It was in November 1983 when I realized I had missed a cycle. I couldn't be pregnant as I was doing my best to prevent it. So I went to the doctor. He had wanted to do a pregnancy test, but I said no, that I had done a home pregnancy test, which I did, and it was negative.

"Those can be wrong, Ms. Meyer," the doctor said.

"I know, but I know it's not. I've been taking the birth control pill. I don't want to get pregnant again. Four's enough, and besides, my baby isn't even a year old!" I said laughingly.

"Okay, if you're sure. It's up to you," replied the doctor.

"I'm sure," I said.

So he prescribed me a pill that should start my cycle. "But you aren't supposed to take it if you're pregnant. That's why I'd like to do the test," he said. We didn't have insurance and would have to pay for it, so I declined again.

"Well, take this as directed, and if you haven't started within a week, we'll do a sonogram to see what might be the problem."

"What could be the problem?" I questioned.

"It could be some sort of blockage like a tumor, but don't get worried. It's more likely just a hormonal issue, and this should do the trick."

I started taking the pills as directed. After the allotted time, I still had not started my cycle. So I scheduled a sonogram. I didn't wait long. The doctor was anxious to see what could be the problem. I couldn't be pregnant. After all, I didn't *want* to be pregnant, not with my life the way it was. I felt like I was raising the four girls by myself.

I went to the hospital to do the sonogram. As the technician proceeded with putting the gel on my abdomen, she asked why the doctor was having me do this. "To see if I have a tumor. I've missed two cycles, and the pills I took didn't get me going," I told her.

"Well, let's have a look. I sure hope it's not a tumor, but if it is, we can hope it'll be able to be removed and not be cancer," she said.

Cancer! I hadn't thought of that! What if it was? Well, I'd get it taken care of. I didn't know just how I'd pay for the surgery, but we'd figure it out.

"Are you sure you're not pregnant, Mrs. Meyer?" the nurse asked me as she rolled the instrument around one more time.

"Yes, I'm sure. Why?" I asked a bit worried.

"Well, because your tumor has little arms and legs!" she said with a smile.

"What! That can't be! I've been taking precautions! I just had a baby! I can't be pregnant!" I said in a panicked voice.

"Well," she began again, "that may all be true, but I'm pretty sure it's a baby! Congratulations! Will this be your second child?"

"No! My fifth!" I said as I got up.

"Five! How blessed you are, Mrs. Meyer!" she said and then left the room.

I made an appointment to see the doctor in the next few days. Kendle had asked me to stop by and let her know the results, so I headed toward her house.

Pregnant! Really? I thought as I drove down Apple Valley Road. *I can't be!*

"But you are," God softly spoke to my heart.

"But Loretta is just a baby, and I just can't handle another one. I can't do this anymore!" I began to cry. I felt so overwhelmed.

As I drove into Kendle's driveway, I gathered myself and went to the door. When Kendle answered the door, I blurted out, "I'm pregnant!"

"What? Really? Congratulations!" she said with a smile.

As I briskly walked past her into the house, I said, "Congratulations! Ha! I'd rather have a tumor!"

"Now, Patty, you know you don't mean that," Kendle said as she sat down on the couch and had me sit too.

"Yes, I do! I don't want another baby. Four is enough, especially when I'm practically raising them on my own," I cried.

"But this could be a boy!" she stated.

"Yeah, I guess you're right. It could be, but probably not! Girls is what I have!" I said and then laughed, finally.

"You tell Walt yet?" Kendle asked me.

"I haven't had a chance to. You're the first to know. Won't he be surprised!" I said and laughed again.

We spent some time talking and visiting. Kendle was a very level-headed woman, and I was thankful I came over. I had to get home though, as Denise had Loretta and Crystal, and June and Mandy would soon be home from school.

When I told Denise, she was speechless at first. I laughed and said, "The cat got your tongue? It was a surprise to me too!"

"Surprise?" she started. "More of like *wow*!"

"Yeah, I know. It won't be easy, but what else can I do? I'm having another baby!" I said. We then visited briefly, and I was on my way home to meet the girls when they got home from school.

That evening, when Walt got home, I reluctantly told him the news. "Pregnant! I thought you said you weren't pregnant," he remarked.

"I did think that. Believe me. It was a surprise to me too," I replied.

Life had taken a sharp turn for us that day. We were really struggling in our marriage, and nothing, not even God, seemed to be helping. Now I was to have another baby. Another little life to be responsible for, to bring up for God, alone. It was so overwhelming. How was I to handle another one?

"Lord," I prayed, "please help me. I just can't do this without you. I fail so miserably. I am constantly angry, and obviously, Walt could care less about becoming a Christian. I just don't know about this."

"I am with you. Remember your verse," God whispered to me.

"Trust in the Lord with all your heart and lean not unto your own understanding" (Proverbs 3:5).

"Yes, and what does the next verse say?" God questioned me.

"In all thy ways acknowledge him and he will direct your paths" [Proverbs 3:6]. Okay, Lord. Okay. I'll trust you. Please show me the way," I said as I fell into a troubled sleep.

CHAPTER 6

It was now 1984, and we had just celebrated Loretta's first birthday along with Crystal for her third. They were only four days shy of being two years apart. That was close enough in age, I had thought, but now this baby and Loretta would only be eighteen months apart. That seemed too close for me. Yet ready or not, I was having another baby in six more months.

It seemed like everything was falling apart around me. I was still following the Lord and attending church faithfully. I was having some fun with my friends and Cousin Kevin, who was still living in our home, but Walt and I seemed so far apart.

We were. He had his life and his friends; I had mine. The only time we seemed to come together was during our weekly gatherings and barbecues. Thankfully, though, the kids seemed happy with all their friends and our many pets. If it wasn't for the girls and loving them, I don't think there would have been much love to be felt around there.

This was the atmosphere at our home as I carried yet another baby in my womb. I had set it up with the doctor to have my tubes tied right after the birth of this baby. I was not going to get pregnant ever again!

"What did Walt say?" questioned Kendle as I told her my plan one day.

"Well, if he wants another baby, let him get pregnant!" I said laughingly. "I'm done. I only wanted four. Now I'm having number 5. That's it! I'm done!"

Later that same day, God spoke to me as I was driving home from visiting with Kendle. He very clearly spoke these words: "What if it's a boy?"

"That would be wonderful! I always wanted a boy," I said.

"Wouldn't you want to try to give him a brother?" the question was asked.

I thought for a moment on that. "With my luck, I'd have another girl. Besides, I only wanted four, and I'll have five."

"What if he dies?" God whispered.

That question was harder to answer, and I couldn't answer immediately. "What if it's a boy and he dies?" God gently asked me again.

"If it's a boy and he dies, I'll still have four. I wanted four," I said, more to convince myself than to convince God.

And that was it. The conversation was over. My decision would stand. I would have my tubes tied, boy or not. I was just so done with all of it. "I'm the only one raising these kids, and I just can't do any more," I said in finality.

So when June 9 rolled around and I went into labor, Walt once again took me to the hospital. It wasn't St. Mary's this time. Since I was having my tubal ligation, they wouldn't do the surgery since they were a Catholic hospital. So we went to Victor Valley Hospital. Kevin watched the girls for me.

It was in the evening, and Mom and Pop Meyer came to the hospital as they had stopped by on their way to Las Vegas. They were so happy to be able to be there. I figured it would be quick, so I thought it wouldn't interfere with their plans too much. I was wrong. It took four hours of hard labor. By the time the baby was coming, I was worn out.

As we went to the delivery room, Walt was getting excited. Mom and Pop went to the waiting room. After what seemed like forever, the baby came, and the doctor announced, "It's a boy!"

"It's a boy, Patty!" shouted Walt. "It's a boy!" He began to rub my head and run back and forth from me to the baby. He had the biggest smile on his face!

"Let me see," I said a bit wearily. Then the doctor held him up, and I saw my precious little boy for the first time.

Walt came over and rubbed my head one more time and whispered, "It's a boy," so lovingly in my ear.

"And what will you name him?" asked the doctor.

That was easy. "Walter Lewis Meyer III," I said. Finally we were able to use the name we had chosen so many years ago. "Little Walter," whispered Walt as he looked lovingly at his new son. Then as the nurse led him out of the delivery room, I leaned back and sighed. "A boy. It's a boy."

I was scheduled for my tubal ligation at nine o'clock the following morning. The doctor said this was best as there wouldn't have to be such extensive surgery since I had just had the baby. If they waited too long, it would be harder and take longer for me to heal.

That night, as I held little Walter in my arms, I felt such contentment. As I laid there holding him, once again, the Lord spoke to my heart. "Are you sure you want to have your tubes tied?" he asked.

"Yes," I answered. "I really don't want to take a chance of getting pregnant again and it not be a boy. He'll just have to be satisfied with four big sisters. But I am so grateful for little Walter, Lord, truly grateful for all my children." God said no more about it to me. I snuggled up to my baby boy and kissed his head as Walt walked into the room to see us with his mom and dad.

The next morning, I had my procedure. The doctor said I would have to stay in the hospital for two more days to help give a good start to the healing process. "You are not to lift anything, not even when you get home. You have a few stitches, and I don't want them to tear open," he instructed me.

"Fine, doctor, but I do have an eighteen-month-old. What about her?" I asked.

"No! Definitely not her for at least a week or two. I don't even want you vacuuming or anything for the first two weeks. All I want you to lift is the new baby," he answered sternly.

"Well, okay. I'll do my best, but I am a mom of four other kids you know," I replied with a chuckle. "I know, I know, but you must listen or it'll take longer, and you could possibly end up back here if you don't take my advice."

"I'll try, doctor. Really, I'll try."

That evening, Walt brought the girls in to see me and their new little brother. It was something new—the hospitals allowing the whole family in to visit. June had just turned nine, Mandy was six, Crystal was three, and Loretta was one. It was also new to leave the baby in the room with you in a hospital bassinet. The only time they took the baby was when you asked because you were tired and needed rest.

My nurse had come and put the baby in my arms and told me my family was on their way to see us. "You have five children?" she asked.

"Yep! Four girls and now a boy, but that's it," I said.

"That's enough. You have your hands full, deary," she said with a chuckle as she left the room.

I was lying down with the baby in my arms when they came in. June and Mandy immediately came to my side to see the baby. "This is your baby brother, girls," I said. "His name is Walter."

"Just like daddy's, huh, Mom?" June asked.

"Yes, just like daddy," I answered.

"See, I told you," June said as she turned her head toward Crystal.

She looked a bit bewildered, so I explained. "Honey, Daddy's name is Walter, and Mommy's name is Patty. You just call us Mommy and Daddy." It didn't seem to make sense to her, but it didn't matter as we all jumped up at a crashing sound.

Walt had put Loretta down when he came over to see the baby. "Walt!" I said anxiously. "Get her before she breaks something." He raced over to get the baby bassinet away from Loretta. She had pushed it across the room and then into the bed next to me. Luckily there wasn't anyone else staying in the room.

"She's just playing. She is just a baby herself," I said. "Lift her up here to see the baby." I told Walt after he got everything back in place.

"Okay. Look, Loretta. That's your new baby brother," Walt said as he leaned her near so she could have a good look.

She smiled a cute smile. Then she started to climb out of Walt's arms into mine, which was still occupied with Little Walter. Suddenly, all four girls decided to climb into bed with me and the baby.

I put my arm over my abdomen where the stitches were and asked Walt to help. "Girls! You can't climb on me! Watch out for the baby!" I was saying as I struggled to keep everyone safe. I had to grab Loretta before she fell to the floor and keep elbows and fingers out of the baby and bodies from crushing my stitches.

"Walt! Do something!" I shouted as I was struggling. He was trying but just didn't know where to begin. "Come and get the baby. Loretta just wants her mommy," I said as I calmed down and saw the sad look on her face.

Walt came and rescued the baby, and I let Loretta climb up next to me and held her for a bit. Then I held Crystal in the other arm as I explained that mommy had a boo-boo and they couldn't climb up on me for a while. They all were laughing and jumping a bit when the nurse came in.

It had only been a few minutes, but it seemed much longer. "Everything all right in here?" she asked.

"Yes," I answered her.

"We heard a crash in here, and we're down the hall," she said with a bit of concern on her face.

"Oh that!" I said and went on to explain Loretta's little adventure with the bassinet.

"We can't have anyone destroying those," she said sternly. Then a bit more lightheartedly, she said, "You girls like your baby brother?"

"Yeah!" they all chimed in.

"That's good."

Then it dawned on her that all the kids were in bed with me. "You'll have to get down from off the bed," she told them.

"They just want to be near me," I replied.

"You just had surgery and don't need kids climbing in bed with you," she told me.

"That's okay, honey," Walt said. "We need to go anyways. We have to eat still. I was going to go through McDonald's or something."

Walt was doing his best, but this was the first time he had all four girls to handle without me. He looked a bit overwhelmed and tired. I smiled up at him and told him that it was fine if they had to leave. So all the girls came and let me give them a hug and kiss. They seemed sad, but when they heard *McDonald's*, their faces lit up.

"McDonald's!" they exclaimed as they started to jump up and down. "Now be good for your daddy. Bye! I love you!" I said as the nurse helped move the girls and Walt out of my room. She came back in just a few minutes.

"Are all of those children yours?" she asked.

"Yes they are," I answered a bit wearily.

She went on to say, "That's a beautiful family. What are their ages?" So I told her their ages. "And now you have your boy. You'll have your hands full, though, especially with the eighteen-month-old. She's just a baby herself."

"I know. That's why I let her climb up on the bed." She just smiled and said I'd better get some rest, that the baby would be waking up and needing fed. So I let her place little Walter in the bassinet and fell into a tired sleep.

The next day was the surgery, and I had only Walt and a couple of friends for visitors as I was in need of rest. I was to be discharged the next day as our medical coverage allowed only a three-day stay, and that was an extra day because of surgery. Yet when my doctor came in the next morning on his rounds, he asked if I wanted to stay another day to get more rest.

"Sure!" I said. "I'd love to, but will it be okay?"

"It'll be okay if I deem it necessary," he stated with a bit of a smile. "I'll put it in my chart that you can stay another day." I think he was informed by the nurses of the visit from the kids. Either way, I was grateful for another day of rest.

I was able to be in the hospital a total of four days, and the doctor asked me on the morning of the fifth if I wanted to stay another day. He was definitely having pity on me, knowing what I had to go home to, but I reassured him that I had friends who would help.

"Good," he said. "Because you will need rest. Remember, you had surgery and have stitches."

"I know," I replied. "Denise is going to help as well as others."

Denise was his patient as well, and he knew we were close friends and each other's helpers, so he consented to release me that day.

I had arranged it to have Denise watch the girls while Walt picked me and Little Walter up from the hospital. Walt was so excited when he came. "The doctor asked me if I wanted to stay another day. Can you believe that?" I told him as we waited for the wheelchair.

"Did you want to stay?" he asked me, a little bit concerned.

"No! I miss the girls so much! How are they doing?" I said.

"They have been good for Denise while I was at work. It's been fine usually, but I'll be glad when you're home."

"Well, I have to take it easy. I told the doctor I would, and that's why he released me. I told him I had Denise to help until you get home," I said with a bit of trepidation.

It was obvious to me Walt expected me to jump right back into my usual routine and I would because what else could I do? With my mother up north and my mother in-law sixty miles away, I would have to make it on my own. I had done it with Crystal and Loretta, and I would do it again, but I was grateful I had Denise to help as usual. Walt would try, but it all overwhelmed him. Besides, he would soon return to his usual routine too, one of working hard and drinking much. *Life would not change*, I thought as I sighed deeply, or so I thought. Then we loaded our son into the car seat, and I climbed into the backseat next to him, and we headed home.

CHAPTER 7

The next few months proved me right. Walt was a proud daddy of a baby boy, but, as usual, I was the one who did the care of all the girls and now the new baby. I was the one who always took care of the bills, groceries, and if there were enough funds, I took care of shopping for clothes, gifts, etc. Well, I took care of everything except the earning of the money, the care of the cars, and most of the yard work. Just like all the other families, I guess, but I felt as if I was raising this family on my own.

I shouldn't have felt that way, I realize, but Walt and I were growing so far from one another, and nothing—not even our new son—seemed to help in making our relationship better. Day after day, the bitterness I felt toward Walt and his constant drinking was getting worse. I would go to Lois; sometimes even walking the five miles in the middle of the night; and we would pray, and I would be able to continue for another day or so.

I wrapped myself and the kids up in my friendships and found our fun with everyone else but Walt. Kevin was one who found things to do, and it was a relief for me to have him around. He would come up with ideas that usually were free and came with an adventure.

Like going to the dry Mojave River bed. This river ran under the ground most of the year, so we could go and play around and discover so many things about the desert and sometimes play in the water that came to the surface. Sometimes we'd go to the parks and just let the kids play and have a picnic. I would take little Walter everywhere we went, even though he was just a newborn.

On the weekends, Walt would join us. Most weekends, we would spend it with our friends and my brother, Joe and his family. Having the crowds of people was a mechanism for me to cope with Walt's drinking. Now he wasn't the only one drinking beer the whole time. Occasionally, Joe would, as well as our friends Denise, John, and Rick. Having everyone around made it possible to keep so busy that I didn't have to deal with the drinking.

This seemed to work as I continued down the road of bitterness. I just was so ignorant of where my heart was heading. I continued to follow God's word and what I felt was necessary to be a Christian. I knew that without God, I would not be there. I would not have been alive, for at the time of my salvation I wanted to commit suicide. Well, during these times, suicide was a constant thought. It seemed an easy way out, an escape from Walt's drinking, from the constant feeling of despair. Yet God would not have it, of course, and my children were here and needed me.

The kids were what made life worth living, and I was so grateful that God blessed our sad lives with each one of our children. They were the only joy in our lives, and I surely did not want to leave them to be raised by Walt. Honestly, suicide was just a selfish way out of a battle that I was not letting God have. I just didn't realize that then.

I was doing my very best to be a good Christian and felt I was on the right path, and I was. I was following the Lord in every way possible. I prayed faithfully for Walt's salvation, and surely God would hear my prayers and save Walt. It was getting more and more difficult to keep the victory without him by my side on this path toward heaven.

I did enjoy the crowds of friends, but I took it a bit too far. Donna and Rick had been renting the house that belonged to Terri and Ed Reedy. This was located around the block from our house. Terri and Ed were moving back so Donna and Rick, with their three boys, moved into our eight-hundred-and-twenty-five-

-square foot, two-bedroom, one bath house! I insisted because I felt it was the right thing to do. I felt we should help our friends, even at the expense of our comfort. Besides, it was only for a month so that they could save enough to move to their own place. Oh, and we can't forget that my cousin was living with us as well!

Now, with a total of thirteen people in that size of home, one could see that it might get difficult for us to get along—but it wasn't. Well, I thought it wasn't, but Walt had never wanted to allow it, yet he did see that our friends were in need. I really didn't give him an option other than to let them move in though, as I was done asking and just insisted. So began the next battle in our married life.

When Donna, Rick, and the boys moved in, we all agreed that they would save for an apartment. This would entail first and last months' rent and a deposit. We figured that if they didn't have to pay to live with us—except help with food—that it shouldn't take longer than two months. Both were working, so it was very doable.

Well, that was in August, and come October Walt had had enough. The straw that broke the camels back was when Donna purchased a new cross-country bike and complete riding gear for her oldest son. I was upset about it too, as it cost over a hundred dollars! How could she afford this if she was saving to move? Walt asked me that exact question.

"I don't know! I don't even know why she bought it!" I exclaimed. "Well, she better return it and put that money toward them moving!" answered Walt. "I can't make her do that. Why don't you talk to Rick?" I asked. "I did, and he said it wasn't his idea." So I did confront Donna.

"Donna," I began, "why in the world did you buy that for James?"

"Because he wanted it. Why?" she replied.

"Because you are suppose to be saving to move!" I said exasperatedly.

"Yeah, I know, and we are. James just really wanted this, and I just had to get it for him."

That did it! I was so upset! "You are supposed to be moving out! Not buying expensive things for your kid! I can barely afford the bills around here! If you have extra money, we could sure use some!"

"It's been so hard for James, moving in here. I just wanted to get him something to ease the pain," Donna said.

Ease the pain! Wow! I gritted my teeth and said, "Ease his pain? *Are you kidding?* What about the pain we are all going through? It's not been easy for anyone! What about my kids? As a matter of fact, what about your other kids? Is James the only one that matters?"

"It's my money, and I'll do with it what I want," she replied.

Just then I felt God was not happy with how I was reacting. I had realized that Donna was drifting from God for a while. She was letting go of God. We had talked briefly about that, and she was not going to admit it. Donna was reverting back to the girl I knew in high school. She was becoming cold and stubborn in her attitude.

I then said a prayer for grace in my heart and continued, "I am sorry, Donna. Really! I never wanted you moving here to cause a problem or come between our friendship. We are only trying to help you. Can you see why Walt and I would have a problem with you buying that for James?"

"Well, I guess," she replied, yet she never offered that it was not a good choice or that she would return the items. That was all she said, and I just let it go.

The stress and conflict just continued to build during the next few weeks, and with that Walt's drinking became worse. Even Rick could see it and told Walt to pull back on it. He would not cut back. Instead, the quantity of beer that he drank became dangerous. Finally, Walt told Rick they had to move.

"But how are they going to do that? They haven't saved enough. Maybe nothing!" I asked Walt.

"That's not my problem!" he said. "I want them out! Now!"

"Well, we have to give them some time to find a place," I replied.

"Fine. They can have two weeks and that's all. I want them out of here by then," Walt said.

That meant they had until November 15th. So I informed Donna and said it had to be. We couldn't do this anymore. Our friendships were affected by the stressful situation, as were our kids. So finally, they started to seriously look for a place.

It was on November 12, 1984, that we celebrated our tenth anniversary. We hardly were talking to each other, but we went to dinner with most of our friends. It was a good enough time, and it helped ease the tension that had built around us. We realized, as did Donna and Rick, that it was the best thing for all of us that they move.

With the help of their family, they were able to purchase a small trailer and set up a day to move. It was to be November 18th, using the days prior to clean the trailer and move their stuff in.

On November 17, I was to bake and decorate a cake for Terri's son, Eddie. We had a day full of people, as usual. I was busy all day long and had planned on going shopping with Becky (another dear friend), Kendle, and Donna. We needed some groceries for dinner the next day, which was Sunday. I never shopped on Sunday, so it was a necessity. Becky suggested we do a little Christmas shopping too, but Donna didn't want to.

This disagreement ended up with Donna and Kendle deciding not to go with us. I had planned on taking Little Walter with us and leaving the other kids with Walt and Rick, who were outside drinking in the garage, and Kevin. "Well, if you're not going, do you mind if I leave Little Walter with you guys?" I asked. "It's cold and I know he's not sick, but I don't want him to get sick."

I had taken him to the doctors just two days prior because he had a slight running nose. It had been a constant thing, and I was a little concerned. The doctor checked him over and said he was fine. Donna agreed to watch him even though Walt was there. "Walt's just too drunk to take care of him. Thanks," I told her.

So as I finished telling Walt that the plans had changed and just Becky and I were going, he said he wanted to go. "You're too drunk!" I said. Becky whispered that I should probably let him go and that Donna and Kendle were keeping an eye on the kids. Besides, my cousin Kevin was there, and he hadn't been drinking.

So I reluctantly agreed and went back into the house to tell Donna that Walt was going. As I started to leave, I leaned down and placed Little Walter in the cradle. We had moved it to the living room so we could keep an eye on him while he wasn't in his crib. His crib was in our bedroom as the only other bedroom already had seven kids and one adult in it. Tonight there was even one more kid. Joey was there too—Joe and Kendle's little guy.

As I gently laid Little Walter in the cradle, he reached up with his little hands and cried slightly. I bent down to let him touch my face, then I lightly placed a kiss on his forehead. "I love you," I whispered and smiled down on him. He continued to hold on to my face and look into my eyes. Oh, I did not want to leave! Yet I had to get food for tomorrow. So I kissed him again and said good night.

I gave Donna instructions as to where his bottle was and thanked her for watching him for me. "That's okay," she said. "I'll take good care of him." Then she bent down and took him into her arms and started to cuddle him. I knew she would take good care of him, and besides, Kendle and Kevin were there to help with all the other kids.

Walt was waiting outside and could hardly walk straight. "How is he going to walk through the stores?" I wondered. Well, he insisted he was going, so Becky got into the back seat and Walt started to get in the drivers seat.

"Oh no, you don't!" I said. "You're too drunk to drive, you idiot!" I turned and asked Rick to talk some sense into him. I pointed out that they had drunk three cases of beer. Rick said Walt had drank over two of those by himself.

"She's right, dude," Rick said. "You better let her drive."

"Awww! Fine," Walt replied.

I told Rick "Thanks" as we shut the doors and drove off to the stores. Our first stop was Kmart. We were just going to look around a bit. Walt and I had not bought one thing for Little Walter for Christmas, which was just around the corner. I told Walt that as we walked into the store.

As we started to look on the clothes racks, I suddenly looked up and for some strange reason, I took note of the time. It was 7:24. Then I slowly turned to Walt, who was staggering around. He looked up at me at that exact moment, sobered up a bit, then we both simultaneously said, "We have to get back. The baby needs us." We came close and grasped each other by the arms. Then, just like that, Walt let me go and was back to staggering around. We continued shopping, but I felt anxious and wanted to head home, so I told Becky that and we left Kmart.

"But I thought you needed to go to the grocery store too?" Becky asked me as we drove toward home.

"Yeah, I do. I'll just get what I need for now and hurry up," I said.

"Can I get a few things too?" Becky asked me.

"Sure, but let's hurry. I hated leaving the baby. I just want to get back. I feel anxious about the baby for some reason," I told her. So we quickly went through the grocery store and headed home.

Becky loaded her things into her car as I went into the house. "How's Little Walter?" I asked Donna.

"We were going to go out so I put his coat on him, but he was real fussy and crying for his bottle, so I got up to give it to him, and he just fell asleep in my arms," she said.

"Aw! Poor little guy! He must have been exhausted. I'm sorry. I hope he wasn't too much problem," I told her.

"No problem. I just laid him down on your bed," she replied.

"How were all the other kids?" I asked. "Kevin kept them in the bedroom and they're sleeping. Or at least I think they are," Donna offered.

So, as I walked back to take care of Little Walter and put him in his crib, I checked in on the other kids. They seemed to be asleep, and I teased Kevin with "Did they wear you out?" as he was lying down too. He said he was tired and would see me tomorrow.

So then I went to my bedroom, but when I got there, I just didn't want to disturb Little Walter. "Poor guy! You were just so tired!" I whispered as I looked down on him. It was so cold in my bedroom because our large window, which came almost to the floor, had a huge hole in it—and it was November. Even in the desert, it gets cold that time of year. I decided to leave him there on our bed. I needn't cover him because he had his coat still on. I thought about removing it but decided not to. So I pulled a sheet on top of his legs for a bit more warmth.

I went back out and told Becky everything was fine and thanked her for going with me. She then thanked me and said good-bye and drove on home.

I turned and went back into the house. Walt had already staggered back into the garage, where Rick and Joe were doing their "partying," and grabbed another cold can of beer from the case he just bought from the grocery store. This made the fourth case Walt had started drinking, and I believe he was the only one drinking at that time. He had actually drank nearly three cases by himself. It's amazing he wasn't near death.

As I entered the house, Kendle was putting on her coat and getting ready to leave. "You have to leave now?" I asked. I was hoping we could visit a bit more, but I knew it was getting late.

"No, we have to get home. It's past ten o'clock, and Joey is needing to get to bed, and so does Joe for that matter—and me!" Kendle said. "We'll see you guys later. Thanks, Donna, even though we didn't get to go to the store," she said to Donna with a smile.

"No problem. Maybe next time," replied Donna.

"You should have gone with us," I said. "No, we just decided to go after you were gone, but Little Walter fell asleep anyways so we couldn't go," Donna offered.

"I'm sorry! I should have taken him," I said.

"He was obviously tired so it was good you didn't take him," Kendle said as she gathered Joey together and headed for the door.

"Yeah, I know, and thanks for taking care of him for me," I replied.

"Don't thank me, thank Donna. She has the magic touch," Kendle said with a smile again as she walked outside, calling for Joe to come on.

We all went outside to say good-bye to Joe and Kendle. As they drove away, I said I had better get back in and finish the cake I was decorating for Eddie. I planned on making a picture of a cheering crowd and a football going over the goal post.

Walt said he was going to get another beer and went into the garage to get it from the fridge out there. Rick followed him, saying that maybe he ought to call it quits for the evening.

"Naw man!" Walt slurred. "I'm just getting started!" Rick let out a slight groan and followed Walt into the garage, and Donna and I went back into the house.

After working on getting the cake frosted, I had started decorating it. Just then, Rick came into the kitchen. "Patty," he started. "You better move the baby off the bed. I think Walt's about ready to pass out," he said a bit wearily.

"He finally came back in?" I said sarcastically.

"Yeah, but he can't walk anymore so I think he'll fall into bed as soon as he gets out of the bathroom," offered Rick.

"Fine. You're right. I wouldn't want him to fall onto the baby and smother him," I said jokingly yet disgusted at the same time.

I looked at the clock to see what time it was because I wanted to finish the cake before midnight. It had been a long night already, and I just wanted to finish and go to bed myself. It was nearing eleven, so I quickly wiped my hands off with a towel and left to go put the baby into his crib.

I entered the cold, dark bedroom but didn't turn on the light because I didn't want to wake the baby. I then picked up Little Walter from off our bed. He was lying on his stomach, as was the

customary way to lay babies then. He seemed stiff, but I attrib-
uted it to the coat he still had on.

He also seemed a bit light. *Strange,* I thought for a brief
moment. I then turned him around as I held him up in my arms.
I brought him to me to kiss him on his cheek. "Oh, I love you,
buddy," I said and then I kissed his cheek. It was cold. I squinted
to try to see his face as the light came in from the hallway. I
sensed something was wrong, so I slowly walked into the hallway.

As my eyes adjusted to the light, to my horror, I looked onto
the cold dead face of my baby boy! There was blue all around
his mouth. His sweet mouth, that just a few hours earlier I had
kissed. His face was distorted and his arms were stiff and straight
out. Those little hands that reached up and held my face were
now ice cold. As a matter of fact, he was completely cold! I felt
my being crumble inside as I realized that my baby, my sweet
baby, was dead.

I tried to scream but only a deep gurgle sound came out. I
was screaming, inside myself, and fell against the wall as my legs
started to collapse underneath me. I was screaming at the top of
my lungs, or at least trying to—but Kevin called out asking, what
was wrong, and didn't we think it was time for bed? I tried to
speak but couldn't! I couldn't do anything! I could hardly hold on
to Little Walter, but I couldn't drop him! My head was spinning!
I couldn't breath!

Just when I thought I couldn't manage holding on to him or
my sanity anymore, Rick came around the corner. "Man, what
now?" he asked, thinking Walt was stumbling around. I quickly
jerked my head around to face him. I'm sure he saw the horror on
my face. "What?" he continued. I tried to talk but couldn't. I just
grabbed all my strength and stood up, still holding Little Walter.
Rick looked bewildered. I still could not speak! I turned the baby
to face him and ran at him with Little Walter right in front of
me, making a groaning sound all the way!

Rick fell backward into the television as he saw what was
the problem. I stopped and laid the baby down on the floor at

Donna's feet. That's where Rick and Donna slept, on our living room floor. Donna sat up then and rubbed her eyes, asking what was going on as I ran into Rick's arms.

Still unable to speak, I just looked up at Rick, who then pushed me gently away and ran to where Donna was grasping in the situation. He cried out to Donna, "What do we do?" Donna then started mouth-to-mouth resuscitation on Little Walter. I looked up and saw Kevin coming out of the bedroom just then.

"What's going on here?" he questioned. He then took in the grim situation. I still could not speak a word. My head was spinning, and a wave of emotion overtook me! I grabbed a chair and started to throw it through the sliding glass door! Just as it was coming around, Rick grabbed it and placed it back down.

"We have to call the police guys!" Kevin was saying as he grabbed the phone. I ran over and yanked it out of his hand and tried to remember how to dial. Out of pure frustration of not being able to remember who to call in an emergency and no one finding the number in the phone book, I started to beat the phone off the wall with the receiver.

I was then finally able to scream out. "*This stupid phone!* Why won't it work?" I questioned as I looked at the phone as it barely hung there. Kevin then turned and ran out the door.

Rick gripped my shoulders and asked me, "Where's Walt?"

"Oh my God! I haven't told him yet! He's in the bathroom!" I wailed.

"Go get him! Does he know Little Walter died?" Rick asked again.

"I don't know. I'll go see," I said as I ran to the bathroom. All this time, the other kids were in the bedroom.

I pushed the bathroom door open and Walt was sitting on the toilet, oblivious to what was going on out in his living room. "Walt!" I choked. "Little Walter is dead, honey." He looked up at me, and I thought he was getting up so I ran back out. I ran to Donna, who was working on the baby. I then ran to the front door, pulled it open, and screamed for Grandma Debbie, who lived across the street from us. I figured she had helped me when my kids were sick, maybe she could help now. I was obviously not thinking straight. There was no way she could have heard me and most certainly couldn't have helped.

Leaving the front door wide open, I ran back to the kitchen and saw that no one was getting anywhere with the phone. Rick then turned and, looking around the living room, asked where Walt was.

"What?" I said. "I told him." Then I ran to the bathroom again and pulled open the door. This time I screamed at him. "*Walt! What are you doing? Little Walter is dead!*"

He looked up and smiled at me. I then grabbed him up by his shirt and screamed directly into his face. "*Your son is dead, you idiot! Get out here!*" Then I threw him down on the toilet and ran out once again.

As I ran and stood over my dead son, I looked up as my neighbor Jim came to the opened door. He was a policeman, and I knew if there was any chance of resuscitating my son, Jim would know how. He stood there for a brief moment with a look of horror on his face, then he plunged into my living room.

Finally! I thought. I then ran outside. As I did, I stopped and turned to my garage door and started to beat it with my fist. I beat it until my knuckles started to bleed. Just then, Kevin came running into our yard. He was the one who remembered that our neighbor was a policeman, and he used their phone to call the emergency squad.

Kevin grabbed me then. Thinking I could fall apart now, I fell into his chest for a brief moment, but he turned and ran into the house. Just as he did so, Walt—finally aware of the situation—came running out of the house.

"*Patty!*" he screamed as he grasped me tightly, by my arms. "Little Walter is dead!" he moaned as he shook me forcefully.

"I know! I found him!" I cried as I started to lean into him, expecting him to hold me. He just threw me away from him and ran back into the house!

There I was, alone in my grief! No one to hold me. No arms to fall into and cry. I was completely by myself with my unbearable sorrow. I started to spin around. My head was spinning, my heart was dying, and I could not breathe anymore. Where was everyone? Why was I alone? How was I to function?

Suddenly, I ran to the middle of the yard and crumbled to my knees. As I buried my face into the cold, wet grass, I screamed, "*God!* I need you, and I need you now!" I demanded as I pounded my fist in the grass in front of me. I looked up then and said once again "Now!" and pointed to the grass. Some may think that almost sacrilegious, but it was pure, honest desperation that made me call out that way.

Instantly, I felt his presence. I sensed he was hovering there above the ground in front of me, holding Little Walter in his arms. I fell to the ground again and prayed that God would bring back my son to life. I knew, beyond any doubt, that God could do just that.

"God," I started to pray within myself, "I know you can bring him back to life. You are God! Please, God! Please!" I begged. Then I prayed, "But only if it's your will. I do want your will to be done."

Just then, I sensed him leaving with my baby in his arms. "*No!* Wait, God!" I screamed out, and God came back to the same spot before me. "If you bring him back to life, just think of how it will help all those people in there believe in you!" I plead silently with him. "But only if it's your will," and instantly he was leaving once again.

"Please, God!" I began again. "Walt would truly believe if you brought Little Walter back to life. Not to mention Rick, Kevin, and the emergency people. Surely you want them saved, don't you?"

Nothing.

My face then fell back into the dewy grass, and I sensed him hovering there.

"God, this isn't fair!" I cried. "I've done everything you've ever asked of me, or at least tried. He's my only son!" I cried again.

"I know all about that," God answered me.

"Yes, but I'm not you. This is too hard for me to do. I can't let him go! I want him alive!" I silently cried.

God so patiently waited as my breaking heart came to terms with his will. "If it's not your will, then I really don't want him back, but I'll need help, Lord. I'll need your help to let him go," I whispered in anguishing prayer.

"I'm right here, child" he whispered back into my heart.

"God," I was crying out again as I beat into the ground. "I'm so mad! I don't understand it! I'm not mad at you, but I'm so completely angry!"

"I know, child," he gently said.

I was completely exhausted now. God went on, "I was so mad when my Son died that I shook the whole earth!" That's when I realized God did understand. He explained, "You're angry at death. Sin is the reason we have death in this world."

"You're right," I whispered. "It is death I'm mad at, and, God, you are the one that overcame death. I will see my son again and hopefully, so will Walt. I will need you to help me now, but take Little Walter and let him know how much I love him, please," I said as I got up from the ground.

"He knows," God whispered as I sensed him leaving with my son cradled safely in his arms. I also sensed Little Walter looking at me with his beautiful eyes and a smile on his face. "I love you, honey, and Mommy will miss you, but you're safe with Jesus now, and I'll see you soon," I whispered as I let go of my only beloved son.

I took a deep breath, wiped the tears from my face, and went into the house. My family would need me. Walt was losing it, and there were my girls and Donna's boys still inside. What were they thinking and going through as the drama unfolded before their young eyes? I was needed inside, and I would have to be strong.

CHAPTER 8

As I entered my living room, I could see my son's body on the floor with a white sheet over him. I knelt down to remove the sheet and kiss him one last time. "No! You don't want to do that, Mrs. Meyer," the EMT told me. I looked up and saw the look of pity on his face. So I laid down next to my baby and just held him.

I was going over the lines in his face when suddenly a man said, "Good grief! That's enough! Get the body out of here." I looked up and realized I had been outside for most of the time and was unaware of what had been going on in here.

So I got up and as they started to take the body up, Walt screamed out. "No! You can't take him!" And he reached out for the gurney.

"That does it!" said the man who had said it was time to get the body out. "I want him arrested!" he shouted.

What? Was he kidding? "Who are you?" I shouted at him.

"I'm the coroner!" he shouted back at me.

"Well, you may be that, but he is the father of the dead baby, you jerk! He just lost his son! What do you expect him to act like?" I screamed at the top of my lungs.

"Well, he's drunk! He could hurt himself or someone else in the state of mind he's in." the coroner went on. "Officer, you had better make sure everything's safe around here."

"Don't worry. I'll handle it," the chief of police was saying as he held me back from punching the man!

"Does you husband have any guns?" he questioned me.

"Yes, but they're not loaded," I replied. "That may be, but you must get them out of the house. The coroner is right. Your husband and you have just gone through a traumatic experience and you can't be too safe," he said. So I walked out the sliding glass door to where Joe and others were. Kevin had called Joe and Kendle and informed them of the situation. So Joe came back while Kendle stayed home with Joey. I told Joe to get all of Walt's guns and take them to his house.

I then turned back into the house and asked where the girls were. "What?" the coroner asked. "There are more children here? What are they doing here?" he asked.

"They live here," I said, completely fed up with his attitude. "Well, children don't need to be around this. Get them out of here."

It's not like we planned this! I was thinking to myself.

"There must be someone's house they can go to," the coroner was saying.

I looked to Kevin. Just then, Grandma Debbie said, "Denise! She'll take them." I too knew I could count on Denise, so Kevin volunteered to take them to her house. "I'll go to my house and call her and let her know they're coming," Grandma Debbie said as she walked out the door. So it was settled. The coroner insisted that the children couldn't come through the living room, so we had them climb out through their bedroom window and out to the car.

As things settled down a bit, I walked outside to see the gurney being slid into the ambulance. Then as they drove away, Walt and I finally held one another and cried. Just then Walt's parents drove up with his brothers, Billy and Donny. Everyone was now there. Earlier, as the message got around by phone, Brother and Sister Plants had come. I was so grateful for their support as I wasn't getting it from Walt.

He let me go then and ran to his mother. "Son!" his father said as he put his arms around Walt and Mom. Just then, I walked up to them and tried to join in. Suddenly, Walt let go and walked away from me. He started to walk down the road.

"Poor Walt. Go get him," someone said.

"No! Let him go, if that's what he wants!" I said bitterly. I wasn't going to run after him. I had had enough of him pushing me away! Enough of no one being there for me! Poor Walt! What about poor Patty?

Finally I walked down the street and screamed, "*If you leave, don't come back! I don't need you! You're never there! Never!*" I vehemently said. I turned around and saw the look of shock and disbelief on his mother's face.

I didn't care what anyone thought. I was done! I too had lost a son. I was the one who found him dead! I was the one who kissed his cold cheek, and I was the one who had to scream it to his father that his son was dead—not once but twice, before it sunk into his drunken skull!

Walt turned around then and slowly came back. I wasn't waiting. I went back into the house where the chief of police came to me and said he had a few questions for me. He informed me that he had already talked to Donna, but it was imperative he speak with me.

He first reassured me that even though the questions may seem harsh, he had to ask them. He told me then that he personally didn't suspect me, but this was the normal procedure in a case where the baby died suddenly. He even informed me that he wouldn't be surprised if the cause of death was determined SIDS, Sudden Infant Death Syndrome.

"Why do you say that?" I asked him.

"Because if it was suffocation, his mouth would've been blue," he explained.

"It was!" I stated.

"That was pooling of the blood from being face down," he informed me. "With suffocation, the inside of the mouth gets blue, and your sons mouth wasn't like that. Now please forgive me for having to ask these questions at a time like this, but I must."

"No! Please don't be sorry. Ask me anything. If there is anything you can find out as to what killed him and what might help prevent it from happening again, then ask away," I said. So as he began by asking when I found him dead, I told him shortly after eleven. (Later, from the autopsy report, I'd find out that the time of death was determined to be between 7:20 and 7:30. Walt and I had the strange feeling that our baby needed us at 7:24!) I answered every question the best I could.

Finally, after all the police and emergency squad was gone, Brother Plants offered prayer as we all gathered around Walt, who was sitting in his chair, silent and completely exhausted. Joe left shortly after prayer, and the Plants shortly after that. Kevin had left with the kids, and Donna and Rick had headed out to their new place they were going to move into the next day anyways. Whatever happened with the cake I was decorating, I don't know. I didn't know, or feel, much of anything at that time.

Mom and Pop were leaving with Donny and Debbie, but Bill stayed there for moral support. It was very difficult for Bill. Not only because he had to see his brother grieving, but it was his twenty-fifth birthday. This was no way to be celebrating, and I know his heart was hurting beyond words as well.

Time seemed to stand still. Walt and I finally fell into our bed. It was most difficult for me as that was where Little Walter had laid only a few hours before. What time it was, I had no idea. We must have fallen asleep as I woke up after what seemed only minutes.

"I just had a dream, Walt," I started. "I saw Little Walter." He turned over and looked at me. I went on, "I saw him in a bright white crib clothed all in white. He was reaching out for my face like he always did. I bent down and reached out for him, but I couldn't touch him." I was so thankful for that dream. I knew he was at peace with Jesus.

"I want to see him," Walt cried. "Please ask God for me, will you, Patty?"

"I'll pray about it, but it's up to God. You need to ask too. Maybe if you pray, God will answer," I told him.

"You pray and I'll pray along with you," he said. So I did pray and asked God to let Walt see Little Walter somehow, if it was his will.

"Do you think he will answer?" Walt asked.

"Oh! He'll answer. He always does," I stated. Then I continued, "It's just sometimes no. I don't know what God will do. You just have to trust him, Walt. Now let's go back to sleep and we'll see. It might not be tonight."

So we fell back to sleep. When we woke up this time, the sun was coming up. I yawned and sighed as I got out of bed. I was looking into the crib, which was in our bedroom next to our bed, when Walt woke up. He got up slowly, and as he did he looked a bit bewildered.

"He did it, Patty! He did it!" Walt said as he came to a full standing position. He then grabbed me and hugged me.

"What?" I questioned him "He did?"

"Yes!" Walt exclaimed. "God answered my prayer! I saw Little Walter!"

"You did!" I exclaimed under my breath. "What did you see?" I questioned him further.

"I saw Little Walter playing on the grass, and he was with Jesus!" he said. "It was far off, but I could tell it was him. I could see him so clearly, and he was so happy. I know he's okay. Thank you, honey, for praying," he said to me.

"You prayed too, you know. Thank God for the answer," I replied.

"Oh, I do thank God!" he said with such awe. "I do thank God."

We then walked out to the living room. Bill was there, and we thanked him for staying. "I really miss the girls," I told Walt.

"Me too," he said. \

"Let's go get them. I need to hold them," I said.

"What will you say to them?" Bill asked.

"The truth. We always tell the kids the truth. Little Walter is dead, but he's in heaven and we will see him again," I replied. We then drove to Denise's and picked up the girls, who were quite upset and saddened.

"Mommy," started Mandy, "Is Little Walter sick?" she asked.

"Well, he's more than sick, honey. Girls, your little brother died last night. He went to be with Jesus in heaven," I told them.

They looked at me with bewildered looks. June and Mandy cried and said they wanted to see Little Walter again. "You can when you get to heaven," I replied.

"Will I get to go to heaven?" Mandy asked with a choked-up voice.

"Yes, if you love Jesus and follow him, you can. Just not too soon, okay?" I said as I held onto her. I then reached out and pulled all four girls into my arms.

"Oh God," I pleaded in my heart, "give me the grace I need for my little girls."

Later that day, people from church brought over food. I asked how they found out and they said Brother Plants announced it during service. "Oh! I missed church!" I exclaimed. "I'm sorry!"

"Don't be. No one expected you to be there," the dear sister reassured me.

"Oh! I guess not!" I stated and then laughed. That laugh sounded so strange. Why was I laughing at a time like this, and I think the sister was thinking the same thing as I noticed a strange look come over her. She then quickly excused herself and left.

I walked around in a daze the rest of that day. Walt just sat in his chair and never said a word. He only got up to go lie down. He was in a state of shock and despair, and would remain in that same state for quite a while thereafter. I would lie down and fall asleep on the floor, next to the chair whenever he was there, just to be close to him. I needed him to just hold me and let me fall apart, but he wasn't able to.

Others tried to comfort me, but I was being the strong one once again, so I accepted any encouraging words and all the love from everyone, but my heart was broken, and I thought I could count on Walt to help me. When he couldn't, I just continued to go through the motions, to make a show of strength—but I felt so lost.

CHAPTER 9

The next few days were a blur. We had to go make arrangements for the funeral. Brother Plants would officiate the service, and a neighboring church would allow us to use their sanctuary as our church was so small. Walt's parents came up to watch the girls and give moral support. I was grateful as the girls were feeling very lost in all of this grief.

Walt said he didn't want to go pick out the plot and casket. "I just can't do it," he moaned. "It's too hard for me."

"What makes you think it's any easier for me?" I said.

"We have to do this, Walt," I said, grievously.

"Take Bill. He can help you" was his reply. Bill looked at me with fear in his eyes.

"Bill will go for you, won't you?" mom said, looking at Bill.

"Well, yeah but Walt," he said as he turned to look at his brother. "You have to go. You need to be there and make the choice, not me!"

"You're right, Bill." I said. "Walt, you're just going to have to come. He was your son after all."

"I know that!" he shouted at me.

"Look, we don't need to fight over this. Honestly, Walt, just come. I need you too," I said with a heavy heart.

"You do?" was his reply.

Really? I thought to myself. "Why wouldn't I need you?" Then I said, "Yes. I need you. I can't do this without you." We then fell into each other's arms, and for the first time, I felt Walter's love once again. It was a love full of grief, but love nonetheless.

So we went to the Desert Valley Memorial Park. The funeral director was very considerate and handled the situation, and us, with much care. It was very helpful to have Bill there as well. We first had to pick the casket. They only had two styles of infant caskets. One more simple and a bit less cost; another with a pillow, a bit nicer and cost more. They came in two colors, white and blue. We said we didn't care what it looked like, and we didn't. We told him we didn't even want to be picking one out, but we were sure we wanted it in blue.

"I completely understand," he said and continued. "But I have to show you, and you might think one better suited for your son than the other. We won't have to go into the room with all the caskets. We can bring them out in the hallway, if you'd rather." We told him we'd prefer that, so as he left to get help moving the caskets, Walt and I sat silently and held hands.

After a couple minutes of silence, I said, "I don't care if it has a pillow or what it looks like. I just want to get this over with."

"Me too," said Walt. Bill sat silent. I'm sure he didn't know what to say.

Finally, we were taken out into the hallway. At the end of it were two small caskets.

"These are the two styles. Just take your time. I'll be in my office when you're ready or if you have any questions," he gently stated. As he left, the three of us stepped closer and looked down into these little boxes that were made to fit a baby. How do you decide what to put your baby in to be put in the ground? My heart broke even more, if that were possible.

As we came closer, I noticed the one with the pillow. "He has to have a pillow, honey. For his sweet little head to rest on," I said in a hushed voice.

"Yeah, I think so too," Walt said.

"I don't care how much it cost. He has to have a pillow. It looks real soft inside too," I said, but neither of us would reach in and feel it.

"Okay," Walt said. "Let's tell him we want this one."

After we informed the director what choice we made, he then took us outside to choose the resting spot for Little Walter. They had a special area for infants and children. We were shown a plot that was near a pine tree. It was also right next to the Catholic area. "My mom will like that," I said. We chose the one near the tree. It was close to the driveway so we could find it easier.

Next we had to choose the headstone. We walked around and looked at some of the infant headstones. There was one that said *Safe in the Arms of Jesus* with a lamb engraved on it.

"That's the one!" I said. "He is safe in the arms of Jesus."

"Yeah!" Walt said. "I want that one too."

"If you notice, some have a special vase that can be purchased as well," the director said.

"Oh! Can we get it, honey?" I asked Walt. "I want to be able to keep flowers out here for him."

"I don't see why not," he said.

We went to the office and finished the paperwork and signed over the life insurance policy we had on Little Walter, which was just enough to pay for everything. The director then showed us some memorial cards to choose from for the service. I wasn't pleased with any and asked if we could make up some of our own. "Yes you may, but I'll just need them the day before the service to have them to hand out. We also have these bookmarks that will have the newspaper's obituary. You can have up to six but can purchase more if you choose. We'll need to go over what the newspaper will say," he said. So we had one more difficult responsibility for that day, but we finally finished.

We were so emotionally worn out by the whole ordeal, yet there was still one choice we had to make for his burial. We had to choose what to bury Little Walter in. Walt didn't want to bring himself to help decide on what to bury his son in, so I had too. "I want to bury him in what he died in. I can't bear to see that any more." His clothes had been given back to us from the coroner's office in a bag.

"But I liked seeing him in that coat," Walt said sadly.

"Me too, but that's what he was wearing when I picked up his stiff dead body! I can't bear to see it anymore!" I cried. So it was decided to bury him in his blue-footed pajamas with his diaper and his coat. So mom Meyer and I went to the laundry mat to wash them. Funny, but I just couldn't bring myself to wash them at home.

The next day my parents arrived. It was so good to have them there. Now I didn't have to be so strong. My mom just wrapped her arms around me and cried. Dad hugged Walt as his eyes teared up too. Walt and I both just sobbed in their arms. "We're so sorry" was all they could say. It was all anyone could say.

Each day seemed to be running into one another. We had gone to the printers to see if they had any memorial cards we could choose from. They had the same choice as the funeral home did. I wasn't sure which picture I would use, but I knew what verse I wanted. I had read it in the gospel of Matthew the night before: "But Jesus said, Suffer little children, and forbid them not, to come unto me: for of such is the kingdom of heaven" (Matthew 19: 14).

"Suffer the little children to come..." I stopped at that point and whispered to God, "Suffer them to come. It is suffering, Lord. It's killing me even though I know he's with you."

"I understand, child," he whispered back to me. "It isn't easy I know." Then I felt his love encircle me, and I could move on.

I was agonizing over the small choice they had in pictures. None of them spoke to my heart, and I just had to have it right. Just as Walt said that I had to make up my mind because we had no more time, I was about to give up and choose the typical picture of Jesus as the shepherd holding a lamb. Suddenly, I noticed *the* picture! It was Jesus gently holding a lamb, but up close to his face, and his look was so loving! It was a print of a painting by "Ruth B. Beck"

That was the picture I chose. There was only one, and the printer wasn't even aware of where it came from, but I knew. I knew that God saw that this was very important to me, and he arranged for it to be there. I am so sure of that!

We couldn't afford to get them in color, so we had to just have them copied. It had to be done quickly, so we weren't able to get the typical credit card–sized one. We were able to choose a colored paper stock, so we chose light blue. We had the picture of Jesus centered and the verse placed underneath. Above we had *In Loving Memory of our son; Walter Lewis Meyer III; June 9, 1984 – November 17, 1984.* Only five months and eight days old. My sweet baby! How I still miss him!

It had been determined that the cause of death was SIDS, so we could now move on with the funeral. That was to be my very first funeral I ever attended. Wow! I never expected my first funeral to be that of my own child!

I had asked our friend Terri Reedy to sing the song, "He Came Special Delivery" for I felt Little Walter had come special delivery wrapped up in love. It was a closed casket because we just couldn't bear the thought of our baby being embalmed. There were so many people that the large church was full. I was surprised by how many of them I didn't know. I was also surprised to see the fire and police department represented too. It made me realize just how little I knew of Walter, for these were his friends.

As we sat in the front with our parents on either side of us, God came. I knew he would, but he was there in a way I hadn't experienced before. There was a special presence. An atmosphere of peace and holiness. I was so grateful to God for that. I would need it in more ways than I had anticipated. As the service came to an end, everyone walked past the casket and some turning to extend their condolences. Walt wouldn't look up, so I did and smiled and thanked them.

Then it was our turn to walk past the tiny blue casket. First, my parents walked out into the isle and around front with the four girls following, then me, then Walt with his parents following him. We didn't stop for long by the casket. Why linger? He was gone. His body was there, but he had left with God those few nights prior. Finally, we walked outside.

Walter and I were standing there looking in as the pallbearers picked up the little casket and carried it toward the door and us. My dad took the girls to his car, and I turned to watch as the casket was placed gently into the back of the Hurst. I thought Walt was right there with me as I took a step closer. I was saying my final good-byes in my heart when I felt weak. I turned to take Walt by the arm for support, but he was gone.

I looked all around but could not see him anywhere. Becky came to my side and took my arm as she fell apart and started to cry. "I just can't believe he's gone," she cried.

"I know," I said as I tried to console her.

"I know he's not my son, but it hurts me so much!" she offered. "I know he's with Jesus, though, and you will see him again."

"That's right," I said. Then I asked her where Walt was. "I don't know. He wasn't here when I walked up," she stated. So I started to look for him and could not find him anywhere. "Anyone know where Walt is?" I asked out loud to no one in particular. I heard someone say they saw him with his mom and dad.

As I wondered about, lost and feeling all alone, I realized I didn't know what to do next. I never thought about it, but who was I supposed to go with? What was next? I saw my mom standing there watching me with a look of sheer sadness on her face. "You can come with us, Patty. Your dad took the girls, but there's room for you." She must have seen how lost I felt.

I thought for a moment, then I decided to go with my husband, even if he couldn't be supportive of me. So I thanked my parents and told the girls I loved them and reassured them we would be together at the grave site and that it would soon be over.

Yet how could this ever be over? I thought. Then I climbed into the back of Walt's parents' car, and finally the procession to the grave site was on its way.

As we drove down Main Street, escorted by the police, the clouds parted, and you could see the clear blue sky. The sun shone in beams down on the earth as all the vehicles pulled into the memorial park. We all gathered around the grave site, which was set up nicely with a few chairs covered by an awning and a carpet of fake grass covering the hole that would soon be the resting place of my baby. I sadly looked at Walt. He too was thinking the same thing. June looked at it as well then at me. I just smiled and said it would be okay. Then, thankfully, the service started once again.

Brother Plants gave the last testimony and prayer. All our friends and family who were able to come walked by and extended their condolences. When I saw a friend I hadn't seen in a while, I smiled brightly and felt happiness. Once again, it seemed strange to be happy at a time like this, but I was. Walt, on the other hand, could barely look up, let alone even speak to anyone.

That's how the worst day of my life went. Walt sat in silence while I greeted those who came to our house afterward, smiling and thanking everyone. This being my first funeral, I didn't know what was expected of me, but I didn't care. I just had to keep moving or I'd fall apart. It would be months before I could ever fall apart, and then it was because I decided it was my turn.

I lost all sense of time. It seemed like time stood still. I'm not sure just when, but maybe a couple of weeks had passed after the funeral when my friend Tami and her kids were there visiting us. I wasn't sleeping very well.

After that dreadful night, the first week, we had all the girls sleep with us in our bed. They needed us, and we needed them—not to mention I was so fearful of finding one of the girls dead that I could not sleep through the night. I would wake up and have to see if everyone was breathing, even when they were back in their own beds.

Anyway, this night was no different. I had woken up and went to check on the girls. This time though, I could not go back to sleep. Finally, in the hours just before sunrise, I got up and went out to the kitchen and sat at the table.

I started to cry as I sat there by myself. Just when I got myself a piece of paper, I don't know. How long I was there, I don't know. I just started to pray and cry out in my heart to God.

"Why?" I questioned. "Why my son?" Donna had asked me if I had thought that God took Little Walter because of sin in my life. "No!" I said. "I know everything is clear between my heart and God. Besides, death would happen if I was a Christian or not. Having God in my heart just makes it bearable." Then I thought, *What is she thinking about?* Then I put it out of my head.

Now, though, I was thinking about it. "God, what about it? Is there something I'm not seeing? Have I sinned and that's why?" I asked as I lay my head on my arms in front of me on the table and started to cry. How long I cried I don't know, but suddenly, I lifted my head and started to write.

The words just flowed onto the paper. Word after word, line after line, a poem emerged on the paper. As I wrote, the tears flowed, and my heart filled with awe. God was giving me the answer. I read what was on the paper and could not believe it. It was exactly all the emotions I had been going through. The bewilderment, the anger, the anguish, and finally the acceptance. God was so merciful to me. I can only praise him for how he stood by me and held me through it all.

Life after Death

Grief has stricken its blow, sorrow fully came.
My infant son has died. For me, life would not be the same.
The anguish I felt, I cannot explain.
It was from deep within and without measure it came.

Just when I thought I could no longer stand
My friend came to me and said, "I understand."
"Understand!" I retorted. "Why this cannot be!
Your arms are not aching! The cradle is not empty!"

Gently He took me and turned me towards Him
"Look up for the hope so your life won't be dim."
"Hope! There is none! You do not understand!
My son died when a baby, yours grew to a man!"

"Look up!" my friend cried. "Please look to me.
Understand? Yes, I do. It is you who cannot see.
My Son had no cradle. His bed was made of straw.
My baby so tender, had no comforts at all.

Aching arms I have not known, is what you say of me.
Yet many children I have lost. Yes, I know such agony.
Yes, my Son grew to a man. Only to be crucified!
As He hung on that tree. Oh! How I had cried!

So you see, my child, I do understand.
Now will you look to me? Will you take my hand?"

So slowly I looked up into the face of my Lord.
My spirit was melted and into His arms I was poured.

"Oh, gentle Father! Now I can see! Your Son is Jesus who
    died for me.
This pain, we felt. This agony, we share. With You as my
    strength I will no longer despair.

Yes, my infant son has died and life will not be the same
For praise the Lord! The Comforter came!"

Right after I had finished reading what I wrote, Tami came into the kitchen, yawning.

"What's up?" she asked me.

"Look," I said as I handed her the sheet of paper.

As she read, she sat down at the table with me. "This is good, Patty! What made you write it?" she said.

"I couldn't sleep and came out here. I was praying, then I started to write."

"No. This was God," she said.

We just sat there for a moment in awe, then we got ourselves a cup of coffee and started another day. I was used to going through the motions of life now, but Walt still was not.

CHAPTER 10

It would be three months or more when Walt went through each day with minimal effort. He continued to go to work and come home, but he would hardly speak to me or the girls. His drinking continued, although a lot less. Finally, I could stand it no longer and confronted him about it.

"Walter, I need to talk with you," I started one evening after dinner. The girls were in their room playing, and Walt was headed for his chair to zone out in front of the television again.

"What?" he said.

"You have to snap out of it," I said in earnest. "I can't do this alone anymore. I need to cry and grieve, but someone has to be here for the girls. It's not fair to them. They've lost a brother and are hurting too. I've been here for them while you zoned out, but I can't hold on much longer. I need to grieve!"

Walt just looked at me at first. What he was thinking, I don't know, but suddenly, he snapped out of it. "Okay," he said.

"You mean it?" I replied. "You can be here for the girls while I let go?"

"Yes, I can. I will," he said.

He then took me by my shoulders and drew me to his chest. I could hardly believe it. Was he really holding me? I had given up hope for us. I was contemplating divorce that dreadful night. I felt there was no hope for us because we weren't happy with one another and neither of us was going to be the one to change.

We had been told that when a child dies, it could make the marriage or break it. That's because both parents need to grieve, and they do that in different ways. Where we were prior to our son's death, you'd think we'd be at each other's throats, but that's not at all how it was. God had a plan.

I had continued to hold on to God, and Walt, not having a relationship with God, withdrew to himself. God knows our hearts, and he knew and understood Walt's grieving as well as mine. He knew just when it was time enough for me to be strong and Walt needing to withdraw and when it was time to switch.

As he held me in his arms and I could feel his strength once again, I collapsed for the first time since that awful night. Finally I could cry, and I did. How long, I'm not sure, but I was grateful that Walt was pulling through, and I knew we would make it. God had brought us through to the other side of death, and life would never be the same again.

I fell apart after that while Walt became the pillar of strength for me and the girls. I was grieving in ways that I was unaware of. Once, I woke up unable to open my mouth. My teeth were clenched, and they stayed that way. I couldn't even fit a fork through them, so I went to the dentist.

He took x-rays and told me there was no physical reason that he could see for the problem. He asked if I was in any pain.

"No," I replied.

"Strange," he said as he tried to pry my teeth apart. Then he asked if I was under any stress.

"No, nothing to be stressed about," I started. "Well, my son died, but that was over three months ago. I'm fine now."

"I'm sorry," he offered. "What happened?"

I filled him in on how my son died of SIDS. "I was the one who found him dead," I said in a hushed voice. "I check on my other children every night."

"Well, that would do it," he said, and then gently, he explained that I was still grieving and was clenching my teeth tightly through the night. In doing so, I had acquired lockjaw. "I will give you a mild tranquilizer to help you relax and sleep." My heart skipped a beat.

"But what if it happens again?" I asked.

"What?" questioned the dentist.

"One of my kids die!" I answered anxiously. "I'll need to be able to wake up!"

"These won't make you sleep that hard, and besides, your husband is there too, right?"

"Yes, he is, and he's doing much better now. At first, I was the one who needed to be strong for the other kids. After three months, I finally told my husband it was my turn to cry."

"You're absolutely right. Now try these for a couple of days, and if it doesn't go away, call me."

It only took three days, and I could open my mouth. Who would have thought that would happen because of grieving? Certainly not me.

I would like to say that our marriage got better; it did not. We had a reason to stick together now more than ever before, but that did not take the place of love. We had drifted so far apart from one another that even this tragedy could not draw us together. We made our marriage work, but life was becoming a vast wasteland, even to the point that our girls were sadly affected.

Yet God had brought us through such a life storm. We had survived the "Santa Ana Wind Storm" of our desperate lives. Just like those winds of the High Desert that blow at such high speeds that it wipes the fields of all life and such relief when it's over, God brought a relief to our marriage. Not a complete healing yet. That would come in time. First, the bitterness had to be blown out of my life, and God, in his great mercy, knew just how to do that.

I looked up into the face of my Lord that night and found hope, peace, and assurance that my life would go on, and I would be a witness for him. I even felt sure that through the tragedy, Walt would come to God and live for him. Surely he would want to go to heaven now to see his son once again. It wasn't to be that way, and my heart hardened with each new rejection from Walt. Not just rejecting me but rejecting Christ. I tried in every way possible to get Walt saved.

How could I have thought that way? I was so ignorant! It would never take me or my efforts! It had to be all God. I just thought I knew how to help. Later in life, I would find the answer in Acts 17:30, and it would help me understand that God understood my ignorance. It says, "And the times of this ignorance God winked at; but now commandeth all men every where to repent" Even though I meant good, my efforts were selfishly driven. God's mercy was poured out on me and Walt for years to come. We had been married only ten years, but life had changed in many ways. Now God had to change our hearts and the wastelands of our lives.